BODMAS Blast Off: A Fun Way to Master Maths

Rekha Kumari

Published by rekharaj, 2024.

While every precaution has been taken in the preparation of this book, the publisher assumes no responsibility for errors or omissions, or for damages resulting from the use of the information contained herein.

BODMAS BLAST OFF: A FUN WAY TO MASTER MATHS

First edition. April 2, 2024.

ISBN: 979-8224168699

Written by Rekha Kumari.

Table of Contents

Dedication

To the curious minds and adventurous spirits,

In a world where numbers dance and equations sing, this book is dedicated to you. You who see math not just as a subject, but as a universe waiting to be explored, an adventure waiting to unfold.

May these pages be your launchpad, propelling you into the boundless realms of mathematical wonder?

May they ignite the spark of curiosity within you, guiding you through the labyrinth of numbers, operations, and puzzles?

Let this book be your trusty companion on your journey to mastery, your compass in the vast landscape of mathematical concepts. With each turn of the page, may you discover new horizons, unlock hidden treasures, and unravel the mysteries of BODMAS.

Here's to the dreamers, the thinkers, the problem-solvers, and the mathematicians in the making. May this book be a beacon of light on your path, illuminating the way to understanding, clarity, and triumph?

For the love of numbers, the thrill of discovery, and the joy of learning, embark on this adventure with us. Let's blast off into the cosmos of mathematics together!

With boundless enthusiasm and infinite possibilities,

Rekha Kumari

The Lady Entrepreneur & Educator

<u>Legal Disclaimer</u>

Copyright@Rekha Kumari - 2024

The publisher and the author disclaim any liability for any damages or losses arising directly or indirectly from the use of this book.

All information contained herein is offered for entertainment and educational purposes only and does not constitute professional advice or instruction.

Names, characters, places, and incidents are either products of the author's imagination or used fictitiously.

Any resemblance to real persons, living or deceased, or to actual events is purely coincidental.

Publication of any part or any moral or lesson for commercial uses is strictly prohibited.

Artificial Intelligence Disclaimer

Copyright@Rekha Kumari - 2024

While the story and illustrations within this book were created with the assistance of artificial intelligence, the core concept, plot development, and overall message originated with a human author.

The purpose of this AI integration is to explore the potential of artificial intelligence in creating engaging and educational content for children.

This disclaimer clarifies that AI was used as a tool in the creative process, but the core ideas and themes are from a human author.

It also emphasizes the book's focus on educating children about the potential of AI.

Preface

Hey there, space cadets and future math whizzes!

Have you ever looked at a math problem and felt like you were staring at a jumble of numbers from another planet?

Fear not!

This book is your rocket ship, ready to take you on a thrilling adventure where learning feels like... well, anything but a chore!

Get ready to:

- **Meet the BODMAS Crew!** Captain Bracket, Officer Of, Sergeant Times, and the rest of this wacky bunch will be your guides on this cosmic journey. They'll show you how BODMAS (Brackets, Of [Multiplication and Division], Multiplication and Division [left to right], Addition and Subtraction [left to right]) is the key to cracking any math code!

- **Embark on Exciting Missions!** From escaping asteroid fields to fixing robots and planning intergalactic parties, each chapter throws you into a fun story packed with BODMAS challenges.

- **Solve Problems Like a Pro!** Don't worry, you won't be left adrift in the mathematical void. **Engaging activities** like board games, puzzles, and creative projects will help you master each BODMAS rule with ease.

- **Unlock the Secrets of Everyday Math!** Did you know BODMAS is used everywhere, from shopping for snacks to building the coolest treehouse on the block? This book will show you how!

Albert Einstein once said, "The important thing is not to stop questioning. Curiosity has its own reason for existing."

Well, this book is all about keeping that curiosity alive!

So, grab your spacesuit, buckle up, and get ready to blast off into a world of fun and mathematical mastery with BODMAS Blast Off

Rekha Kumari

The Lady Entrepreneur & Educator

Open Talk with Rekha Kumari

Hey little learner!

As the author of BODMAS Blast Off, I'm incredibly excited to share this book with you and your amazing kids. Now, I know what you might be thinking: "Another math book?

Isn't that, well, kind of...boring?"

Here's the thing – it doesn't have to be!

BODMAS Blast Off!

Is a bit of a **milestone** because it takes something that can feel overwhelming (order of operations!) and turns it into a **wild space adventure**.

Think of it this way: mastering BODMAS is like having the key to unlock a whole treasure chest of math problems. It's the secret code that helps you solve anything from figuring out how many cookies you can share with your friends to building the tallest tower ever!

But sometimes, just holding the key isn't enough. You need a fun map to guide you, right?

That's where BODMAS Blast Off! Comes in. With its quirky characters, exciting stories, and awesome activities, this book makes learning BODMAS feel like a **blast** (pun intended!).

So, why is this a milestone?

Because it shows that learning math can be **engaging**, **imaginative**, and even **downright fun!**

We can ditch the boring drills and worksheets and take a more **adventurous** approach.

I truly believe that every child has the potential to be a math whiz, and BODMAS Blast Off!

Is here to help them unlock that potential. So, are you ready to join the BODMAS crew and become a master mathematician?

Let's blast off!

Rekha Kumari

The Lady Entrepreneur & Educator

Chapter 1: The BODMAS Bunch Assemble!

Have you ever heard of the most terrific, most mathematically marvellous crew to sail the seven seas of numbers?

Well, gather around, me hearties, because I'm about to introduce you to the BODMAS Bunch!

Our captain, a fellow both brave and bold, was none other than Captain Bracket!

He wasn't your typical captain with a fancy hat and a parrot on his shoulder.

No, sir!

Captain Bracket was a square-rigged kind of captain, always there to keep the order and make sure everything was shipshape... or should I say, equationshape!

First mate and always by his side was Officer Of. Now, Officer Of wasn't much to look at. He was a skinny little fellow, more like a colon than a full-fledged officer, but don't let his size fool you!

Officer Of had the sharpest mind on the crew. He could sniff out a misplaced operation from a mile away and always knew the proper order of things.

Then there were the twins, Sergeant Times and Corporal Division. These two were thick as thieves, always seen together, their voices booming like a pair of cannons.

Sergeant Times was a burly multiplication sign, always flexing his muscles and shouting orders. Corporal Division, on the other hand, was a slender fellow with a diagonal slash across his chest. He was much calmer than his brother, but don't underestimate his cutting wit!

Rounding out the crew was Miss Addition, the sweetest lady you ever did meet. With a plus sign for a smile, she could add up a mountain of numbers in the blink of an eye. And don't forget Minus Minus, the grumpy old subtraction symbol. He always seemed to be subtracting his good mood, but deep down, everyone knew he cared.

Together, this oddball crew, the BODMAS Bunch, sailed the high seas of mathematics, solving problems, cracking codes, and always making sure every equation was squeaky clean!

Let Us Learn the Lesson

The full form of BODMAS is:

- **B - Brackets**
- **O - Order of (powers and roots)**
- **D - Division**
- **M - Multiplication**
- **A - Addition**
- **S - Subtraction**

BODMAS stands for **Brackets**, **Of (powers and roots)**, **Division**, **Multiplication**, **Addition**, and **Subtraction**. It's a fancy way of remembering the order in which we solve a math problem when there are multiple operations involved. Here's a breakdown of what each letter represents and why the order matters:

B - Brackets:

- Anything inside brackets needs to be solved first. They act like little shields, protecting their contents until we deal with them.

O - Order of (powers and roots)

- This one can be a little tricky! Before we move on to multiplication and division, or addition and subtraction, we need to tackle any **powers (exponents)** or **roots** in the equation. Remember, a power is a number raised to another number (like $2^3 = 8$), and a root is the opposite (like the square root of 9 is 3).

D - Division & M - Multiplication:

- Once we've dealt with brackets and any powers/roots, we move on to division and multiplication. The key here is to **work from left to right**. That means we solve any division or multiplication signs in the order they appear, no matter which comes first.

A - Addition & S - Subtraction:

- Finally, we tackle addition and subtraction, again working from left to right.

Why is the order important? Imagine you have a recipe that says "Add 2 cups of flour, then mix in 3 eggs and 1 cup of sugar." If you added the eggs and sugar to the flour first, then tried to measure out 2 cups, your measurements would be all wrong! It's the same with math problems. Following the BODMAS order ensures we get the correct answer.

Here's an example:

Let's solve the problem: 2 + 3 x 4 - (10 ÷ 2)

Following BODMAS:

1. **Brackets:** We have a bracket first, so let's solve what's inside: (10 ÷ 2) = 5
2. **Order:** There are no powers or roots in this case.
3. **Multiplication:** Next comes multiplication: 3 x 4 = 12
4. **Addition and Subtraction:** Finally, we work from left to right: 2 + 12 - 5 = 9

So, the answer to the problem is 9.

By following BODMAS, we ensure we solve the problem in the correct order and get the right answer!

Check Your Basic Knowledge

1. Captain Bracket needs your help navigating an asteroid field! Solve this equation to find the safe path: (5 + 2) x 3 - 1 = ?
2. Officer Of is baking space cookies. She needs to divide 18 cookies equally among 3 astronauts. How many cookies will each astronaut get? 18 ÷ 3 + 2 = ?
3. Sergeant Times is building a robot. He needs 4 bolts for each leg and the robot has 2 legs. How many bolts does he need in total? 4 x 2 + 6 = ?
4. The spaceship needs 8 units of fuel to reach the next planet, but they already have 3 units onboard. How much more fuel do they need? 8 - (2 x 2) + 1 = ?
5. There are 7 friendly aliens on the space station, but 2 need to leave for a mission. How many aliens will be left? 10 - (3 + 1) = ?
6. There are 12 space pizzas on board, but the crew ate 4 before your arrival. How many pizzas are left? (8 x 2) - 4 = ?
7. The spaceship needs to travel 24 light-years, but they can

travel 4 light-years per hour. How many hours will it take to reach their destination? $24 \div (3 + 1) = ?$

8. The robots need to collect 15 moon rocks. They already have 5. How many more rocks do they need to collect? $(2 \times 3) + 15 - 2 = ?$

9. There are 9 planets in the solar system, but scientists recently discovered a new one! How many planets are there now? $8 + (1 \times 3) = ?$

10. The crew needs to collect 20 space crystals. They found 7 blue crystals and 5 red crystals. How many crystals do they have in total? $(7 + 5) \times 2 = ?$

Chapter 2: Brackets to the Rescue!

Our heroes, the BODMAS Bunch, were cruising through space in their trusty ship, the "Equationator," when disaster struck!

They found themselves smack dab in the middle of a swirling asteroid field!

Boulders of rock and ice whizzed past, clanging off the ship's hull.

"Captain!" screamed Sergeant Times, his voice booming through the bridge. "We're trapped!

These asteroids are coming from every direction!"

Captain Bracket, ever the calm leader, gripped his wheel. "Don't worry, Sergeant. We just need to solve the escape code to navigate our way out.

But there's a problem!"

He pointed towards a glowing screen displaying a scrambled equation:

$3 \times (4 + 2) - 1 = ?$

Officer Of, his colon twitching with excitement, piped up. "This is where my expertise comes in, Captain! Brackets take priority, remember?

We need to solve what's inside them first!"

Miss Addition, ever eager to help, jumped in. "Right! So, let's solve 4 + 2 inside the brackets first. That equals..."

"Six!" boomed Sergeant Times, flexing his multiplication muscles.

"Excellent, Sergeant!" boomed Miss Addition. "Now, we multiply 3 by 6."

"Eighteen!" shouted Corporal Division, his slash symbol glinting.

"Almost there!" squeaked Officer Of. "Finally, we subtract 1 from 18."

Minus Minus grumbled, finally finding something to agree on. "That leaves us with..."

Everyone in the bridge held their breath.

"Seventeen!" they all shouted in unison.

Captain Bracket, with a triumphant grin, punched in the code: "Escape code 17!"

The ship lurched and rumbled as it recalculated its route. Asteroids whizzed past them once more, but this time, the Equationator weaved expertly through the field, dodging every rock with mathematical precision.

"We did it!" cheered Miss Addition, a happy plus sign beaming on her face.

The BODMAS Bunch had once again saved the day, all thanks to the power of brackets and their teamwork!

Activity: Matching Mayhem!

Now it's your turn to help the BODMAS Bunch navigate some tricky equations!

Match the scrambled equations on the left with the correct solutions on the right, remembering the order of operations (BODMAS): Brackets, Of (Division & Multiplication),

Multiplication & Division (from left to right), and Addition & Subtraction (from left to right).

Scrambled Equations Correct Solutions

3 x (5 + 1) - 2	16
(2 x 4) + 3	11
8 - (1 + 3)	4
7 x 2 - 1	13
(6 / 2) + 5	8

Bonus Challenge: Can you come up with your own scrambled equation using brackets?

See if your friends can solve it!

Let Us Learn the Lesson

In BODMAS, there's actually only one type of bracket considered, even though we might see them written in different ways. These are typically parentheses (), curly braces {}, and square brackets []. While they look different, they all function the same way in BODMAS:

Grouping and Changing Order:

- **Grouping:** All types of brackets act like little shields, grouping specific parts of a math problem together. They instruct us to solve what's inside them **first** before moving on to the rest of the equation.
- **Changing Order:** By using brackets, we can change the order in which we would normally solve a problem according to BODMAS. Anything inside the brackets takes priority, regardless of other operations outside them.

Why different symbols?

The choice of bracket type is often a matter of **preference or clarity**. Mathematicians might use a specific type depending on the complexity of the equation to improve readability. However, for BODMAS purposes, they all function the same way.

Here's a breakdown of the different bracket symbols you might encounter:

- **Parentheses** ( ) - These are the most common type of bracket used in BODMAS. They are simple and clear for basic grouping.
- **Curly Braces** { } - Less common in BODMAS, these can be used for more complex grouping, especially when there are multiple sets of brackets involved.
- **Square Brackets** [ ] - Also less frequent in BODMAS, square brackets might be used for grouping within grouping, or to set off specific elements in the equation for clarity.

Examples of Brackets in BODMAS:

- **Simple Grouping:**

Let's look at the equation: 2 + (3 x 4) - 1.
Here, the brackets group 3 and 4 together. We solve 3 x 4 = 12 **first**, then add 2 and subtract 1.

- **Changing Order:**

Consider the equation: 8 ÷ (2 + 1) x 3.
Normally, division comes before multiplication in BODMAS. However, the brackets change this. We solve 2 + 1 = 3 **first**, then divide 8 by 3 and multiply by 3.

Tips for Using Brackets:

- Look for any groups of numbers or operations enclosed within parentheses, curly braces, or square brackets. These are your clues that something needs to be solved first.
- Remember, brackets **override** the normal BODMAS order.

Solve what's inside the brackets first, then continue with the rest of the equation according to BODMAS rules.

By understanding how brackets work, you can tackle more complex math problems with confidence!

Remember: No matter the symbol used, all brackets in BODMAS serve the same purpose: to group and prioritize the order of operations within them.

Check Your Basic Knowledge

1. **Space Race Surprise!** Captain Bracket needs your help win the race! Solve this equation to reach the finish line first: (5 + 2) x 4 - 1 = ? (Here, the brackets group 5 and 2 for addition first)

2. **Robot Repair Roundup!** Fix the robot's arm with the right equation. Which one uses brackets correctly? a) 3 x (2 + 4) - 1
   b) 3 x 2 + 4 - 1

3. **Tricky Train Troubles!** A train needs to cross a bridge with a weight limit of 8. Can the train with 3 boxes (each 1 box) and a passenger (2 boxes) cross safely? Write an equation with brackets to find the total weight. (This question tests understanding that brackets change the order – if not used for 3 boxes first, the answer might exceed the limit)

4. **Funky Fruit Fractions!** There are ¾ of a watermelon left and you want to share it equally with 2 friends. How much watermelon will each friend get? (Brackets can be used to group the fraction with multiplication first)

5. **Monster Mash Up!** You need 2 blue potions (each uses 3 drops of a special ingredient) and 1 red potion (uses 4 drops). How many drops do you need in total? (Brackets can be used to find the total used for blue potions first)

6. **Mystery on the Moon Base!** A message is coded! It says: (4 x

2) + 3 - 1 = _ What is the missing number? (Test understanding that brackets are solved first)

7. **BODMAS Olympics!** You're competing in the "Bracket Challenge." Which equation uses brackets correctly? a) 8 - (2 + 3) x 1 b) 8 - 2 + 3 x 1

8. **Planning a Party!** You need to buy 5 balloons (each costing 2 space dollars) and some space streamers for 3 space dollars. How much will you spend in total? (Brackets can be used to find the cost of balloons first)

9. **Building a Treehouse!** You need 4 planks (each 1 meter long) for the floor. Write an equation with brackets to find the total length if you use them all. (Brackets group the multiplication for finding total length)

10. **Shopping Spree with BODMAS!** You have 10 space dollars and want to buy 2 space ice creams (each 3 dollars) and a cool space hat (4 dollars). Can you afford everything? Write an equation with brackets to find out! (Brackets can be used to see if you have enough for ice cream first)

Chapter 3: Multiplication & Division Mayhem in the Milky Way!

On a distant planet bathed in the glow of two suns lived the Zorgons, a race of alien chefs famous for their intergalactic buffets. Today, however, there was chaos in the kitchen of their magnificent spaceship, the "Galaxy Grubber."

Sergeant Times, who moonlighted as the head chef (when he wasn't busy with multiplication!), was throwing his four arms up in frustration. "We've got a triple batch of Zargonian Zlurp to make, but the Gravitation Guacamole recipe calls for exactly 12 Gloop Globs per Zorgonian!

How am I supposed to divide these slimy green globs equally among 8 hungry space tourists?!"

Just then, Corporal Division, ever the calm voice of reason, stepped forward. "Don't worry, Sergeant. This is where my division skills come in handy!

We just need to divide the total number of Gloop Globs by the number of tourists."

Miss Addition, always ready to lend a hand (or rather, a plus sign!), chimed in. "Right! But first, we need to know how many Gloop Globs we have in total."

Captain Bracket, ever the resourceful leader, pointed towards a giant vat bubbling with the bright green goo. "According to the recipe, each batch of Zargonian Zlurp requires 3 Gloop Globs per serving. Since we're making a triple batch, we need to multiply..."

"Three times three!" boomed Sergeant Times, his voice echoing in the vast kitchen.

"Exactly!" beamed Miss Addition. "That's..."

"Nine!" shouted Corporal Division, his slash symbol glinting with pride.

Now, with the total number of Gloop Globs in hand (9), they could finally solve Corporal Division's equation.

"We need to divide 9 Gloop Globs by 8 hungry tourists," he declared.

Suddenly, Officer Of, usually quiet but observant, squinted at the number of tourists. "Hold on a minute! We have one very important VIP guest today – the Grand Gourmet of Glub!"

Sergeant Times scratched his four heads. "Oh no! That changes everything!

We can't just leave the Grand Gourmet out of the Zargonian Zlurp distribution!"

"Don't worry, Sergeant," soothed Corporal Division. "We just need to add one more tourist to the equation. Now, we're dividing 9 Gloop Globs by 9 tourists."

With a flick of his wrist, Corporal Division calculated the answer.

"That leaves us with exactly 1 Gloop Glob per tourist!" he announced.

The Zorgonian chefs erupted in cheers. Thanks to their teamwork and mastery of multiplication and division, they were back on track to create a magnificent intergalactic feast!

Activity: Galactic Grub Dash!

Calling all aspiring space chefs!

Join the BODMAS Bunch on a culinary adventure by playing Galactic Grub Dash!

This board game will test your multiplication and division skills as you race around the spaceship collecting ingredients for the Zargonian Zlurp.

What you'll need:

- Game board with a spaceship path
- Playing pieces (one for each player)
- Dice
- Ingredient cards with multiplication or division problems

How to play:

- Take turns rolling the dice and moving your playing piece around the spaceship path.
- Land on a space with an ingredient card. Solve the multiplication or division problem on the card to collect the ingredient.
- The first player to collect all the ingredients for the Zargonian Zlurp wins the game!

Bonus Challenge: Create your own ingredient cards with fun and challenging multiplication and division problems!

Let Us Learn the Lesson

In BODMAS, multiplication and division go hand-in-hand! They hold equal importance and are tackled together, following a specific rule:

Work from Left to Right:

This means we solve any multiplication or division signs in the order they appear, moving from left to right across the equation.

Why this order matters?

Imagine you have 6 cookies and want to share them equally between 2 friends. If you tried to divide the cookies first (6 ÷ 2 = 3), then multiply by the number of friends (3 x 2 = 6), you'd end up with the wrong answer (6 instead of 3 cookies each).

Following the left-to-right rule ensures we perform these operations in the correct order.

Examples of Multiplication and Division in BODMAS:

- **Simple Multiplication and Division:**

Let's solve: 8 x 2 ÷ 4 = ?
We follow BODMAS and work from left to right: first multiply 8 x 2 = 16, then divide by 4 to get 4.

- **Mixed Operations:**

Consider the equation: 3 + 12 ÷ 2 x 5
Here, we follow BODMAS order:

- We can't solve any brackets or powers/roots as there aren't any.
- We need to tackle multiplication and division next, working from left to right: 12 ÷ 2 = 6, then 6 x 5 = 30.
- Finally, we perform addition: 3 + 30 = 33.

Tips for Multiplication and Division in BODMAS:

- Look for any multiplication or division signs in the equation.
- Remember, they are solved together, working from left to right across the equation.

- Don't jump ahead and solve them out of order.

By understanding this rule, you can tackle problems involving both multiplication and division with confidence!

Check Your Basic Knowledge

1. **Pizza Party Prep!** You need to order enough pizzas for a party. If each pizza feeds 4 people and you're expecting 12 friends, how many pizzas do you need? (Multiplication comes before division)

2. **Space Souvenir Shopping!** You have 15 space dollars and a cool space rock costs 3 dollars each. How many space rocks can you buy? (Division comes before addition)

3. **Sock Situation!** You have 2 drawers with socks. One drawer has 4 pairs of socks and the other has 3 pairs. How many socks do you have in total? (Multiplication is done before addition)

4. **Alien Amusement Park!** The entrance fee is 5 space dollars and each ride costs 2 space dollars. If you go on 3 rides, how much will you spend in total? (Multiplication of ride cost is done before adding the entrance fee)

5. **Sharing Space Cookies!** There are 18 space cookies and you want to share them equally with 3 friends. How many cookies will each friend get? (Division comes before addition)

6. **Collecting Space Crystals!** You find a box with 12 space crystals and your friend gives you another 5. How many crystals do you have in total? (Addition comes after solving multiplication)

7. **Fueling Up the Spaceship!** The spaceship needs 8 units of fuel to reach the next planet, but they already have 2 units onboard. How much more fuel do they need? (Subtraction comes after solving both multiplication and division)

8. **Building a Rocket!** You need 4 bolts for each of the 3 rocket legs. How many bolts do you need in total? (Multiplication comes before addition)

9. **Planting Space Plants!** You have 3 rows for planting space seeds and each row can hold 5 seeds. How many seeds can you plant in total? (Multiplication comes before addition)

10. **Counting Space Creatures!** There are 7 friendly aliens playing outside and another 2 join them later. How many aliens are playing in total? (Addition comes after solving multiplication)

Chapter 4: Times and Division

Building Bridges Together!

On a faraway planet made entirely of metal, lived a crew of friendly robots who loved to build things.

Today, they had a big challenge: constructing a bridge across a giant canyon to connect two bustling robot cities.

Leading the construction crew was Sergeant Times, his usual booming voice replaced by a thoughtful whir. "Alright, my fellow bolts and gears, this bridge needs to be exactly 36 meters long. We have metal beams that are each 3 meters long.

How many beams do we need to complete the bridge?"

Miss Addition, ever the helpful one, chimed in with a series of clicks and whirs. "We can solve this with multiplication, Sergeant! If each beam is 3 meters long, and we need a total length of 36 meters, we just need to find out how many threes fit into 36."

Sergeant Times scratched his metallic head. "But what if the number of beams doesn't come out to a neat whole number?

We can't have half a beam, can we?"

Just then, Corporal Division, his diagonal slash symbol glowing, stepped forward. "That's where I come in, Sergeant!

If multiplication tells us how many sets of things we have, division tells us how many individual things we get when we split a set into equal parts."

"So, you're saying we might need to divide the total length by the length of each beam?" whirred Miss Addition.

Corporal Division gave a satisfied whir. "Exactly! Let's see what happens when we divide 36 meters by 3 meters per beam."

With a series of clicks and whirs, they all calculated the answer.

"The answer is..." boomed Sergeant Times, "...12!"

"That's right!" beeped Miss Addition. "We need 12 metal beams to build the perfect 36-meter bridge!"

The robot crew cheered and set to work, using their combined knowledge of multiplication and division to efficiently build the bridge. By working together, Sergeant Times' powerful multiplication skills and Corporal Division's precise division abilities made them the perfect team!

Activity: Bridge Builder Bonanza!

Calling all junior engineers!

Help the BODMAS Bunch build magnificent bridges by solving these fun multiplication and division problems!

Coloring by Numbers:

- You are given a bridge outline with numbered sections.
- Beside the bridge, you'll see a list of equations with multiplication and division problems.
- Solve each equation!
- The answer to each equation corresponds to a specific color.

- Use that color to fill in the section with the matching number on the bridge outline!

Bonus Challenge: Can you create your own bridge design with numbered sections and write equations that correspond to different colors?

Let Us Learn the Lesson

Building a Bridge with BODMAS!

Imagine you're a brilliant engineer tasked with building a safe and sturdy bridge across a space canyon! To make sure your bridge holds up, you need to use BODMAS just like you would when solving math problems. Here's how:

B - Brackets (Building the Foundation):

- Brackets represent the foundation of your bridge. These could be support structures holding the main beams in place.
- You wouldn't build the bridge on unstable ground, right? So, solving any bracketed sections (like reinforcement beams) would come first, ensuring a solid base.

O - Order of (Powers and Roots) (Calculating Beam Strength):

- This one might not be used as often when building a real bridge. But let's say you're using special space materials with unique properties.
- The "Order" in BODMAS could represent the strength calculations based on the properties (powers) of these materials. You'd need to factor those in before moving on.

D - Division & M - Multiplication (Length and Weight Distribution):

- Division and multiplication become crucial when determining the bridge's length and how much weight it can hold.

- You'd **divide** the total desired bridge length by the length of each beam to see how many beams you need.
- Then, you might **multiply** the weight limit of a single beam by the number of beams to determine the total weight the bridge can safely support.

A - Addition & S - Subtraction (Combining Parts):

- Addition and subtraction come into play when you're assembling the bridge.
- You might **add** the lengths of multiple beams to check if they reach the desired total length.
- In some cases, you might need to **subtract** a small section from a beam to ensure a perfect fit.

Building a Bridge with Confidence:

By following BODMAS, you can ensure your bridge is built in the correct order, with a strong foundation, proper weight distribution, and the right measurements. It's like solving a math problem – each step builds on the last, leading to a successful outcome!

Remember: BODMAS is a guide, and bridge building might involve additional factors. But understanding this concept will give you a solid foundation for approaching any engineering challenge!

Check Your Basic Knowledge

1. **Beam Strength Check!** You're testing the strength of support beams (each rated to hold 10 space rocks) for your bridge. An equation shows how many rocks they can hold together: (2 x 3) + 5 = ? How many rocks can they hold in total? (Brackets group multiplication first)
2. **Planning the Length!** Each bridge beam is 2 meters long and you need a bridge 8 meters long. How many beams do you

need? Write an equation with division to find out! (Remember division comes before addition)

3. **Cable Connections!** You need 4 cables for each support structure (2 structures in total). How many cables do you need in total? (Multiplication comes before addition)

4. **Weight Distribution Worries!** The bridge needs to hold 20 space trucks (each 2 tons) and 5 space buses (each 3 tons). How much total weight can the bridge handle? (Find the weight of each type of vehicle separately before adding them together)

5. **Double-Checking the Base!** You used 3 support beams for the bridge base (each 1 meter wide). Is the base wide enough? Write an equation with multiplication to find the total width. (Brackets can be used for grouping multiplication)

6. **Ramp Adjustments!** The bridge ramp needs to be 5 meters long, but a section might need to be cut to fit perfectly. If you cut off 1 meter, what will the final ramp length be? (Subtraction comes after solving multiplication)

7. **Testing Anchor Points!** Each anchor point (used to secure the bridge) can hold 8 space chains. You need 2 anchor points on each side (2 sides total). How many chains can all the anchor points hold? (Multiplication is done before finding the total number of anchor points)

8. **Light Tower Placement!** You want to place light towers every 3 meters along the bridge. If the bridge is 12 meters long, how many light towers can you place? (Division comes before multiplication)

9. **Painting the Bridge!** You need 2 cans of paint for the bridge base (1 meter wide) and 1 can of paint for each additional meter. How many cans of paint do you need in total for a 5-meter bridge? (Multiplication for base paint comes before finding paint for additional length)

10. **Safety Net Support!** The safety net needs support beams placed every 2 meters. If the bridge is 10 meters long, how many support beams do you need? (Remember division comes before multiplication)

Chapter 5: The Addition & Subtraction Squad Lend a Hand!

On a planet covered in fluffy pink clouds lived the Plorkians, a race of friendly aliens who loved everything to be neat and orderly. Unfortunately, their love for order was being tested!

Their spaceship, the "Cloud Cruiser," was malfunctioning due to a series of scrambled messages filled with addition and subtraction problems.

"Captain Bracket!" squeaked Officer Of, his colon flashing in distress. "The Plorkians are sending a distress signal!

Their spaceship is on the fritz, and they need our help deciphering some scrambled equations!"

Miss Addition, always eager to help, bounced on her toes. "Sounds like a job for the Addition & Subtraction Squad!"

Sergeant Times, ever the show-off, puffed out his chest. "Don't worry, Miss Addition. We'll have those equations solved in a jiffy!"

But when they reached the Cloud Cruiser, they found the Plorkians in a state of utter confusion. Scrambled numbers and symbols were plastered all over the control panel.

"These equations don't make any sense!" wailed a Plorkian with a droopy antenna. "They're all mixed up!"

Minus Minus, who rarely spoke, grumbled a series of clicks and whirs. "It seems their equations lack BODMAS order!"

Captain Bracket, ever the leader, stepped forward. "Don't worry, Plorkians! We'll sort this out together. Remember, addition increases the total, while subtraction takes away. We just need to follow the order of operations!"

He pointed to a particularly confusing equation: "8 + 2 - 1 = ?"

Officer Of, his colon twitching with excitement, piped up. "Since addition and subtraction come after multiplication and division, we solve them from left to right!"

Miss Addition beamed. "So first, we add 8 and 2. That equals..."

"Ten!" boomed Sergeant Times.

"Excellent, Sergeant!" chirped Miss Addition. "Now, we subtract 1 from 10."

Even Minus Minus seemed to perk up a bit at the prospect of subtraction.

With a series of clicks and whirs, they all calculated the answer.

"The answer is..." boomed Sergeant Times in unison with Minus Minus, "...nine!"

Following this method, the BODMAS Bunch, with the help of the eager Plorkians, deciphered all the scrambled equations, fixing the Cloud Cruiser's malfunction. Soon, the pink spaceship soared back into the fluffy clouds, leaving a trail of grateful Plorkians in its wake.

Activity: BODMAS Blast Off!

Ready to build your own amazing spaceship?

Join the BODMAS Bunch in creating a fantastic "BODMAS Blast Off" spaceship using different shapes!

What you'll need:

- Construction paper in various colors
- Scissors
- Glue stick
- Markers
- Cut-out shapes like circles, squares, triangles (enough to build a spaceship)

How to play:

1. Decorate your spaceship with the construction paper shapes.
2. On each shape, write an addition or subtraction problem. Make sure to include some easy and some challenging problems!
3. Once your spaceship is complete, challenge your friends or family to solve the equations and "blast off" the BODMAS spaceship into space!

Bonus Challenge: Can you create your own shapes with even more challenging BODMAS problems that include multiplication and division.

Let Us Learn the Lesson

Addition and subtraction are the final steps in BODMAS, used to combine or separate quantities after we've dealt with brackets, powers/roots, multiplication, and division.

Here's a breakdown of how they work:

Addition (+):

- Addition is used to **combine** two or more numbers.
- Imagine you have 3 apples and a friend gives you 2 more. To find the total number of apples you have now, you would add $3 + 2 = 5$.

Subtraction (-):

- Subtraction is used to find the **difference** between two numbers.
- Let's say you have 5 cookies and eat 2. To find out how many cookies you have left, you would subtract 5 - 2 = 3.

Order in BODMAS:

- We perform addition and subtraction **last**, working from left to right across the equation.
- This ensures we solve all the multiplications, divisions, and bracketed sections first, before combining or separating the final results.

Why the order matters?

Imagine you have 2 cookies and your friend has 3. If you tried to subtract your cookies first (2 - 1 = 1), then add your friend's cookies (1 + 3 = 4), you'd get the wrong answer (4 instead of 5 total cookies).

Examples of Addition & Subtraction in BODMAS:

- **Simple Addition and Subtraction:**

Let's solve: 5 + 2 - 1 = ?
We follow BODMAS:

- No brackets or powers/roots.
- We move to multiplication and division (there aren't any here).
- Finally, we perform addition and subtraction from left to right: 5 + 2 - 1 = 6.

- **Mixed Operations:**

Consider the equation: 3 x 2 + 4 - 1
Here's the breakdown:

- No brackets or powers/roots.
- First, we solve the multiplication: 3 x 2 = 6.
- Then, we perform addition and subtraction from left to right: 6 + 4 - 1 = 9.

Tips for Addition & Subtraction in BODMAS:

- Look for any plus (+) or minus (-) signs in the equation.
- Remember, they are solved **last**, working from left to right after all other operations are complete.

By understanding addition and subtraction in BODMAS, you can ensure you solve problems accurately!

Check Your Basic Knowledge

1. **Space Snack Time!** You have 4 space cookies and your friend shares another 2 with you. How many cookies do you have in total to enjoy? (Addition is used to find the total number of cookies)
2. **Alien Amusement Park Adventure!** You have 10 space dollars and win 5 more playing games. How much money do you have now to spend on souvenirs? (Addition is used to find the total amount of money)
3. **Lost in Space!** You need to travel 12 light-years, but your spaceship can only travel 4 light-years per hour. After 2 hours, how many light-years are left to travel? (Subtraction is used to find the remaining distance)
4. **Packing for the Mission!** You need to pack 3 spacesuits and 2 helmets for the mission. How many items do you need to pack in total? (Addition is used to find the total number of

items)

5. **Fixing the Rocket Engine!** The engine needs 8 bolts, but you only have 5. How many more bolts do you need to find? (Subtraction is used to find the number of missing bolts)

6. **Planting Space Lettuce!** You plant 7 rows of lettuce and your friend plants 3 more. How many rows of lettuce are planted in total? (Addition is used to find the total number of rows)

7. **Building a Space Kitchen!** You need 4 panels for the walls and 2 for the roof. How many panels do you need in total for the kitchen? (Addition is used to find the total number of panels)

8. **Counting Space Tourists!** There are already 15 tourists on the spaceship, and 7 more are boarding. How many tourists will be on board in total? (Addition is used to find the total number of tourists)

9. **Fueling Up!** The spaceship's fuel tank holds 20 units of fuel, but it already has 5 units in it. How much more fuel can the tank hold? (Subtraction is used to find the remaining space for fuel)

10. **Space Race Challenge!** You need to travel 18 space miles to win the race, but your opponent has already traveled 8 miles. How many more miles do you need to travel to win? (Subtraction is used to find the remaining distance to cover)

Chapter 6: Pizza Party Panic!

Disaster struck!

It was Friday night, and Timmy was supposed to order pizza for the biggest movie marathon of the year with his best friends, Sarah, Alex, and Emily. But when he opened the fridge, all he found was a sad, wilted lettuce leaf. Panic surged through Timmy. "No pizza?

What will we eat?!"

Suddenly, a brilliant idea sparked in his mind. He remembered Captain Bracket's teachings about BODMAS from math class. Maybe, just maybe, he could use BODMAS to solve this pizza predicament!

He raced to the phone book and flipped open the page for "Pizza Planet." Looking at the menu, his mouth began to water. Pepperoni for $1.50 a topping, extra cheese for $1.00, mushrooms for $0.75... the possibilities were endless!

But there was a problem. Each friend had different preferences. Sarah craved a cheesy extravaganza, Alex loved a veggie delight, and Emily wouldn't touch anything without pepperoni. How could Timmy order pizzas that everyone would love, all while staying within his budget?

Taking a deep breath, Timmy remembered Captain Bracket's wise words: "Remember, BODMAS keeps the order straight, from brackets down to multiplication and subtraction's fate!"

He decided to create a "build-your-own-pizza" system. First, he'd figure out the base price of a large pizza, which was $8.00. Then, he'd let each friend choose their toppings, keeping track of the additional costs using BODMAS.

The BODMAS Pizza Challenge:

Timmy grabbed some construction paper and markers. He drew four large circles, representing the pizzas for each friend. Beside each circle, he wrote the base price of $8.00. Now came the fun part!

- **Sarah's Cheesy Extravaganza:** She wanted double cheese (2 x $1.00). Using multiplication first (because of BODMAS!), Timmy added $2.00 to the base price. Sarah's pizza now cost $8.00 + $2.00 = $10.00.
- **Alex's Veggie Delight:** He opted for mushrooms and extra cheese, so Timmy had to add $0.75 + $1.00 = $1.75 (remember, addition comes before subtraction!). The total cost for Alex's pizza was $8.00 + $1.75 = $9.75.
- **Emily's Pepperoni Paradise:** She wanted a single serving of pepperoni, so Timmy simply added $1.50 to the base price, making her pizza $8.00 + $1.50 = $9.50.

With a triumphant grin, Timmy dialed the number for Pizza Planet. He proudly relayed his "build-your-own-pizza" order, using BODMAS to ensure he got the correct prices. When the pizzas arrived, dripping with cheese and piled high with toppings, his friends cheered!

Thanks to BODMAS, Timmy saved the day (and the movie marathon) with delicious, budget-friendly pizzas for everyone.

Activity: The BODMAS Pizzeria!

Calling all junior pizza chefs!

It's your turn to run your own pizzeria using BODMAS!

What you'll need:

- Construction paper
- Markers
- Scissors
- Glue stick

How to play:

1. **Create your menu:** On a large piece of construction paper, design your "BODMAS Pizzeria" menu.
2. **Price your pizzas:** Decide on a base price for a large pizza and write it on the menu.
3. **Design your toppings:** Cut out construction paper circles or squares to represent different toppings. Write the price of each topping on its corresponding circle/square.
4. **Take orders:** Have your friends or family "order" their pizzas by choosing their desired base price and toppings.
5. **Solve with BODMAS:** Use BODMAS to calculate the total cost of each pizza, remembering to multiply topping prices before adding them to the base price.

Bonus Challenge: Can you create a special "build-your-own-combo" deal that includes a drink and dessert, with its own BODMAS price calculation?

Let Us Learn the Lesson

Sharing Pizza with BODMAS!

Pizza night with friends is awesome, but how do you make sure everyone gets a fair share? That's where BODMAS comes in! It's a handy tool that helps us solve math problems in the correct order, and sharing pizza is no different!

Here's how BODMAS helps us share pizza fairly:

B - Brackets (Sharing Special Portions):

Imagine you have a friend with a cheese allergy. They can only eat the pepperoni half of the pizza. Brackets could represent this special situation:

(Number of slices for everyone) - (Number of slices for friend with allergy) = Number of slices you can share

O - Order of (Powers and Roots) (Not used in pizza sharing):

This part of BODMAS doesn't usually apply to pizza because we're not dealing with powers or roots (like square roots of slices!).

D - Division (Sharing Equally):

This is the most important part for pizza sharing! We use division to split the total number of slices equally among everyone.

Number of slices / Number of people = Slices per person

M - Multiplication (Sharing Unequally):

Maybe you have a friend with a big appetite! You can use multiplication if someone gets more slices than others.

Number of slices for friend with big appetite = Number of slices per person x Extra slices

A - Addition & S - Subtraction (Combining or Leftovers):

These might come in handy if you have leftover pizza!

- **Addition:** If you have leftover pizza from another day, you can add it to the new pizza for a bigger feast!
- **Subtraction:** If someone doesn't want all their slices, you can subtract those slices from the total to find the remaining amount to share.

Sharing Pizza with Confidence:

By following BODMAS, you can ensure everyone gets a fair share of pizza (or maybe even a little extra for the friend with the big appetite!). Remember, BODMAS is a guide, and sometimes you might not use all the steps. But understanding it will help you tackle any pizza-sharing situation like a champ!

Check Your Basic Knowledge

1. **Pizza Party for Two!** There is a large pizza with 8 slices, and you want to share it equally with your friend. How many slices will each of you get? (This is a simple division problem)

2. **Big Family, Big Appetite!** Your family has a rectangular pizza cut into 12 slices. There are 2 parents and 3 kids. How many slices will each person get if you share them equally? (Division is used to find slices per person)

3. **Allergy Alert!** There's a veggie pizza with 10 slices, but your brother has to avoid mushrooms (half the pizza has mushrooms). How many slices can you and your brother share without the mushrooms? (Brackets can be used to show which slices to subtract)

4. **Leftover Lunch!** There are 4 slices leftover from yesterday's pizza. Today, you order another pizza with 8 slices. How many slices are there in total to share for lunch? (Addition is used to find the total number of slices)

5. **Sharing with the Neighbors!** You bake 2 small pizzas with 6 slices each. Your family of 4 wants 2 slices per person, and you want to share 2 slices with your neighbor. How many slices are left after everyone eats? (Multiplication is used to find the total slices for your family, then subtraction to find leftover slices)

6. **Hungry Helper!** There's a pizza with 16 slices and you call a friend to help you finish it. You agree to give your friend 4 extra slices since they helped. How many slices will you each

eat? (Subtraction is used to find the number of slices you keep after giving some away)

7. **Square Pizza Fun!** You have a square pizza cut diagonally into 8 slices. Your friend insists on getting the corner slices (which are bigger). If there are 4 corner slices, how many of the regular slices are left to share equally? (Subtraction is used to find the remaining slices after taking the corner slices)

8. **Pizza Party for the Class!** There is a giant round pizza cut into 15 slices. You need to share it among 5 friends and yourself. How many slices will each person get? (Remember to divide the total slices by the total number of people)

9. **Double-Checking Slices!** You order 2 pizzas – one with 10 slices and another with 8 slices. Before your friends arrive, you double-check and take out 2 slices to eat. How many slices are left in total to share? (Subtraction is used to find the leftover slices after taking some)

10. **Surprise Delivery!** You baked a pizza with 12 slices, but then your friend surprises you with another pizza with 6 slices. How many slices do you have in total to enjoy together? (Addition is used to find the total number of slices from both pizzas)

Chapter 7: Treasure Hunt Time Travel!

Ahoy, mateys!

Buckle up for a time-traveling adventure with the BODMAS Bunch!

Captain Bracket, ever the daring leader, had stumbled upon a dusty old map in the depths of the Equationator. It wasn't your ordinary map - it was a time travel treasure map! It promised riches beyond imagination, hidden across different eras. But there was a catch - the location clues were all coded messages that required BODMAS mastery to decipher.

"This is a job for the BODMAS Bunch!" boomed Sergeant Times, his muscles rippling with excitement. Miss Addition bounced on her toes, her plus sign practically vibrating with anticipation.

The first clue led them to a scorching desert, a land of towering pyramids and pharaohs. The message on a cracked clay tablet read:

$5 \times (2 + 3) - 1 = ?$

Officer Of, his colon twitching with focus, piped up. "Remember the order of operations, crew! Brackets come first!"

Working together, they solved the equation inside the brackets first: 2 + 3 = 5. Then, they multiplied 5 by 5, getting 25. Finally, they subtracted 1, leaving them with a final answer of 24.

"The clue points to the 24th pharaoh's tomb!" declared Captain Bracket, his eyes sparkling with adventure.

Following the map and their BODMAS skills, the crew traveled through time, facing challenges in each era. They used division to crack a Roman code hidden on a sundial, addition and subtraction to decipher a cryptic message scrawled on a Viking shield, and even used multiplication to solve a riddle whispered by a mischievous court jester in a medieval castle.

Finally, they arrived at their last destination - a bustling futuristic city. The final clue, displayed on a holographic billboard, read:

$(8 / 2) + (4 \times 3) = ?$

Following BODMAS, Corporal Division calculated with precision. He divided 8 by 2 first, getting 4. Then, he multiplied 4 by 3, resulting in 12. Finally, he added 4 and 12, arriving at the grand total of 16.

With a triumphant cheer, the BODMAS Bunch located the hidden treasure, a chest overflowing with... well, that's a secret for another chapter!

The point is, their knowledge of BODMAS and their teamwork led them on an unforgettable time-traveling adventure, proving that math skills can unlock treasures beyond compare.

Activity: The BODMAS Buried Treasure!

Avast, ye scurvy dogs!

Are you ready for your own BODMAS treasure hunt?

Grab a pencil, some paper, and your sharpest math mind, because Captain Bracket has hidden a secret treasure somewhere in your house (or garden, or classroom!).

Here's how to play:

1. Captain Bracket has left a series of clues hidden around your location. Each clue will be a BODMAS equation that needs to be solved.
2. Use your BODMAS knowledge to solve each equation and find the answer.
3. The answer to each clue will lead you to the location of the next clue.
4. Keep solving and following the trail of clues until you reach the final location - the buried treasure!

Bonus Challenge: Can you create your own BODMAS treasure hunt for your friends or family, hiding clues and incorporating fun math problems?

Let Us Learn the Lesson

BODMAS: Your Key to Unlocking a Time-Traveling Treasure Hunt!

Imagine you've stumbled upon a dusty old map promising a hidden treasure!

But to reach it, you'll need to travel through time using a mysterious machine. The only catch?

The machine requires solving BODMAS equations to activate its various functions!

Here's how BODMAS becomes your key to this thrilling adventure:

B - Brackets (Setting the Time Coordinates):

The brackets represent the specific points in time you want to travel to. Numbers within brackets could indicate years, like (1500) for the Renaissance era. Remember, anything inside the brackets needs to be solved first!

O - Order of (Powers and Roots) (Fine-Tuning the Time Travel):

This might not be used all the time, but powers could represent the intensity of time travel. For example, 2^3 (2 cubed) could mean traveling three times further into the future from a specific starting point.

D - Division (Traveling Through Different Time Periods):

Division comes in handy when navigating through different time periods. You might need to divide the total desired travel time by the machine's speed (in years per hour) to find how long it takes to reach your destination.

M - Multiplication (Calculating Time Jumps):

Multiplication is crucial for making specific time jumps. You could multiply the number of centuries you want to travel forward by a factor to reach a precise year.

A - Addition & S - Subtraction (Accounting for Time Differences):

These come into play when considering time zone differences or historical events.

- Addition: Let's say you land in a place 5 hours behind your starting point. You'd need to add 5 hours to your current time.
- Subtraction: If you travel to a time period with a different calendar system, you might need to subtract days to match your starting date.

Solving the Time Travel Puzzle:

The map might provide clues with BODMAS equations! Here's an example:

Start: 2024 / (3 x 2) + [1492] - 100 = ?

Following BODMAS:

1. Solve the division first: $2024 / (3 \times 2) = 2024 / 6 = 337.33$ (This might represent the machine's speed)

2. Then, solve the bracketed year: [1492] = 1492
3. Now we can perform the subtraction: 337.33 + 1492 - 100 = 1830 (This could be your target year)

By following BODMAS, you can decipher the code, activate the time machine, and embark on your exciting treasure hunt through history!

Remember, BODMAS is your guide, and the map might present challenges that require creative thinking and application of these math concepts.

So, are you ready to dust off that map and set off on an unforgettable time-traveling adventure?

With BODMAS by your side, the past (and its treasures) awaits!

Check Your Basic Knowledge

1. **Medieval Mystery!** The time machine can travel at a speed of 5 years per hour. You want to travel back 20 years in total. How many hours will the time travel take? (Division is used to find the travel time)

2. **Pirate Treasure Hunt!** The treasure map says to travel back in time to 1700 (marked in brackets) and subtract 20 years to find the exact year the pirates buried the treasure. What year should you travel to? (Brackets show the starting point, then subtraction to find the final year)

3. **Ancient Egypt Adventure!** You need to travel 3 centuries back in time (each century is 100 years). The machine can multiply the travel distance by a factor. If you set it to multiply by 3, how many years back in time will you travel? (Multiplication is used to find the total number of years traveled)

4. **Dino-Sized Challenge!** The time machine requires a code to activate. The code is hidden in a puzzle: (2024 - 60) x 2 + 100 = ? What is the code? (Brackets are solved first, then

subtraction, multiplication, and addition)

5. **Future Food Fair!** The time machine can travel at 10 years per hour. You want to travel 30 years into the future but need to arrive 2 hours early for the food fair. How many hours total will you spend traveling? (Multiplication is used to find the travel time, then addition to find the total hours spent)

6. **Medieval Mix-Up!** The map says to travel back to 1453 (in brackets). However, you need to adjust for a time zone difference of 5 hours behind your starting point. What time will it be when you arrive? (Brackets show the year, then subtraction to find the adjusted time)

7. **Roman Race Against Time!** You need to travel 2 millennia (each millennium is 1000 years) into the past. The time machine can only travel in increments of 100 years. How many jumps (multiplications by 100) do you need to make? (Multiplication is used to find the number of jumps needed)

8. **Space Station Surprise!** The time machine can travel at 2 light-years per hour. You need to travel back 10 light-years to stop a future space disaster. How many hours will it take? (Division is used to find the travel time)

9. **Viking Voyage** The map says to travel back in time to [1000] and then add 50 years to reach the time of the Vikings. What year do you need to travel to? (Brackets show the starting point, then addition to find the final year)

10. **Jurassic Jungle Journey!** The time machine needs a code to activate. The code is hidden in a message: (2024 - 190) / 2 + 150 = ? What is the code? (Brackets are solved first, then division, multiplication, and addition)

Chapter 8: Tricky Train Troubles!

The BODMAS Bunch were chugging along on a scenic train journey through the mountains. Captain Bracket, sporting a jaunty conductor's hat, was enjoying the view from the engine cabin.

Miss Addition peered out the window, counting fluffy white clouds, and Sergeant Times was busy flexing his muscles, pretending to shovel coal (even though the train was quite modern).

Suddenly, the train screeched to a halt. Officer Of, his colon flashing with worry, rushed into the cabin. "Captain! There's a problem!

The tracks ahead have been damaged by a rockslide. We need to take a detour across some rickety old bridges, but there's a catch - each bridge has a weight limit!"

Captain Bracket's smile vanished. "Weight limit?

But our train has different cars with varying weights. We can't risk overloading any bridges!"

Just then, Corporal Division, ever the calm voice of reason, stepped forward.

"Don't worry, Captain! We can use BODMAS to figure out which combinations of cars are safe to cross each bridge."

Miss Addition's eyes lit up. "That's a great idea, Corporal! We can add the weights of the cars and see if they stay under the bridge limit."

The train conductor, a jolly fellow named Mr. Chuggins, approached them with a worried expression. "Here's the problem," he said, handing them a list. "This shows the weight of each train car and the weight limit for each bridge."

Bridge Weight Limits & Train Car Weights:

Bridge Number	Weight Limit (in tons)
1	15 tons
2	20 tons
3	10 tons

Train Car	Weight (in tons)
Engine	5 tons
Passenger Car 1	3 tons
Passenger Car 2	4 tons
Cargo Car 1	6 tons
Cargo Car 2	8 tons

Captain Bracket stroked his chin. "Alright, crew!

Let's use BODMAS to save the day!

Remember, addition helps us find the total weight of the cars crossing each bridge."

Following Corporal Division's instructions, they started calculating. They figured out that the engine (5 tons) + Passenger Car 1 (3 tons) = 8 tons, which was well under the 15-ton limit for Bridge 1.

They continued using BODMAS for the other bridges, ensuring the total weight of the cars never exceeded the bridge limit.

By working together and using their BODMAS skills, the BODMAS Bunch successfully navigated the rickety bridges, proving that math can be a lifesaver (or in this case, a train-saver!)

Activity: Bridge Crossing Brainteaser!

Calling all future train conductors!

Help the BODMAS Bunch ensure safe passage across the tricky bridges by solving these weight limit puzzles!

Materials:

- Cut-out train cars with different weights written on them (based on the story or your own variations).
- Cut-out bridges with weight limits written on them.

How to play:

1. Place the train cars and bridges on a flat surface.
2. Use your BODMAS skills to figure out which combinations of train cars can safely cross each bridge without exceeding the weight limit.
3. Remember, addition helps you find the total weight of the cars crossing the bridge.

Bonus Challenge: Can you create your own train cars with different weights and bridges with varying weight limits?

Write BODMAS equations to represent safe combinations of cars for each bridge.

Let Us Learn the Lesson

Tricky Train Troubles: Solving Problems with BODMAS at the Train Station!

Imagine you're at a bustling train station, excited for your next adventure. But uh oh, there seems to be some trouble with the trains!

Don't worry, BODMAS (a fancy way of saying the order of operations) can be your hero and help you solve these tricky train problems!

B - Brackets (Grouping Specific Trains):

- Brackets can represent groups of trains traveling together or connected for a special trip.
- You might need to find the total weight of these trains (important for safety) before considering other trains.
- Remember, anything inside the brackets needs to be solved first!

O - Order of (Powers and Roots) (Not Used Here):

- This part of BODMAS doesn't apply to train problems because we're not dealing with powers or roots (like square roots of trains!).

D - Division (Sharing Resources):

- Division can be helpful when figuring out how many people each train car can hold, or how much track each train needs if there are multiple trains traveling on the same route.
- We divide the total number of people (or track length) by the number of train cars (or trains) to find the amount per unit.

M - Multiplication (Calculating Total Numbers):

- Multiplication comes in handy when you need to find the total number of passengers on a trip if there are multiple train cars, each carrying a certain number of people.
- You can also multiply the number of trains by the speed (in kilometers per hour) to find the total travel time for multiple trains going the same distance.

A - Addition & S - Subtraction (Combining or Finding Differences):

- Addition is useful for finding the total number of passengers on a platform if there are people waiting for different trains.
- Subtraction can help you determine how many more seats are available on a train if some are already occupied.

Solving Train Troubles with BODMAS:

Here's an example of a tricky train problem:

(Weight of 3 cargo trains) + (Weight of 1 passenger train) - 200 tons = Maximum safe weight for the bridge

Following BODMAS:

1. Solve the bracketed section first: Find the total weight of the cargo trains (weight of 1 cargo train x number of cargo trains).
2. Then, add the weight of the passenger train to the total cargo weight.
3. Finally, subtract 200 tons (the safety limit) to find the remaining safe weight for the bridge.

By following BODMAS, you can ensure the trains operate safely and efficiently, and your exciting adventure gets underway!

Remember, BODMAS is a guide, and the specific problems you encounter might not use all the steps. But understanding these concepts will help you tackle any train station challenge that comes your way!

Check Your Basic Knowledge

1. **Express Train Trouble!** The express train can carry 120 passengers per car. There are 3 train cars attached. How many passengers can the express train carry in total?

(Multiplication is used to find the total number of passengers)

2. **Platform Panic!** There are 50 people waiting for the local train and 30 waiting for the express train. How many people are waiting on the platform in total? (Addition is used to find the total number of people)

3. **Heavy Cargo!** A cargo train can carry 50 tons of goods per car. There are 2 cargo trains. How many tons of goods can they carry together? (Multiplication is used to find the total cargo weight)

4. **Tunnel Time!** A passenger train is 100 meters long and a cargo train is 80 meters long. What is the total length of both trains if they need to enter the tunnel together? (Addition is used to find the combined length)

5. **Ticket Trouble!** A one-way train ticket costs $10. You and your friend both need tickets. How much will the tickets cost in total? (Multiplication is used to find the total cost)

6. **Snack Time on the Train!** You bring 3 boxes of cookies with 10 cookies each on the train. How many cookies do you have in total for the journey? (Multiplication is used to find the total number of cookies)

7. **Empty Seats!** A train car has 50 seats and 20 passengers are already on board. How many empty seats are available? (Subtraction is used to find the remaining seats)

8. **Double-Decker Dilemma!** A double-decker train car can hold 80 passengers on the lower level and 60 on the upper level. What is the total passenger capacity for the car? (Addition is used to find the total number of passengers)

9. **Bridge Weight Limit!** The bridge can hold a maximum weight of 200 tons. A passenger train weighs 50 tons. How much more weight can the bridge handle before reaching the limit? (Subtraction is used to find the remaining weight

allowance)

10. **Speed Challenge!** Train A travels at 60 km/h and Train B travels at 80 km/h. If they both travel the same distance, how much faster is Train B compared to Train A? (Subtraction is used to find the speed difference)

Chapter 9: Funky Fruit Fractions!

Our heroes, the BODMAS Bunch, were hurtling through space in their trusty ship, the "Equationator," when a distress signal blared through the speakers. Captain Bracket, ever the responsible captain, steered the ship towards the source.

On the screen appeared a group of colorful aliens with bulbous heads and antennae. "Help us, brave space travelers!" squeaked the lead alien, his voice high-pitched. "Our spaceship's malfunctioning, and we can't figure out how to share our fruit harvest equally!"

Miss Addition, ever the helpful one, piped up. "Don't worry, little aliens!

We can help you share your fruit with fractions!"

Sergeant Times, ever the show-off, puffed out his chest. "Fractions? Easy as pie... well, almost as easy!"

The aliens looked even more confused. "Pie? Fractions?

What do you mean?"

Captain Bracket chuckled. "Don't worry, Sergeant. Let's explain. Fractions help us divide things into equal parts."

He pointed towards a screen displaying a vibrant image of the aliens' fruit harvest: a giant pile of juicy space-mangos, some whole, some sliced in half.

"We need to figure out how much fruit each alien gets," explained Officer Of, his colon flashing with thought. "But there's a problem! Some aliens have bigger appetites than others."

Just then, Corporal Division, his diagonal slash symbol gleaming, stepped forward. "That's where BODMAS comes in!

We can use it to solve equations involving fractions and ensure everyone gets a fair share."

Miss Addition bounced on her toes. "Sounds like a job for the Funky Fruit Fraction Squad!"

The aliens' eyes widened with wonder. They had never seen such a colorful and enthusiastic crew.

The BODMAS Bunch, with the help of the eager aliens, set to work. They used addition and subtraction to combine fruit portions, multiplication and division to distribute fruit slices fairly, all while following the BODMAS order.

For example, one equation involved sharing 3 whole space-mangos among 4 aliens. They divided 3 wholes by 4 aliens, resulting in ¾ of a space-mango for each alien (remember, division comes before multiplication!).

Another equation involved giving 2 aliens each ½ of a space-mango. They used multiplication first (BODMAS!), giving each alien a total of ½ x 2 = 1 whole space-mango.

Soon, the entire fruit harvest was divided equally, with each alien holding a happy handful of space-mangos. The aliens cheered, showering the BODMAS Bunch with grateful words and promises of delicious space-mango smoothies.

With a satisfied smile, Captain Bracket patted the control panel. "Looks like we've restored order to the fruit harvest, and all thanks to BODMAS and a little teamwork!"

Activity: The BODMAS Fruit Fair!

Calling all young mathematicians!

Join the BODMAS Bunch in running a fantastic "BODMAS Fruit Fair" where everyone gets a fair share!

What you'll need:

- Construction paper in various colors
- Markers
- Scissors
- Glue stick
- Cut-out shapes of different fruits (circles, squares, etc.) with whole numbers written on some and fractions written on others.

How to play:

1. Decorate your "BODMAS Fruit Fair" with the construction paper and fruit cut-outs.
2. Imagine you have a set number of players (pretend they are aliens!). Write that number on a separate piece of paper.
3. Now comes the fun part! Use the fruit cut-outs to create BODMAS equations involving fractions.
    - You can use whole fruits to represent whole numbers.
    - Use fruit slices (like halves, quarters) to represent fractions.
4. Challenge your friends or family to solve the BODMAS equations to figure out how much fruit each "alien" would receive at the fair.

Bonus Challenge: Can you create your own BODMAS equations with fractions that involve more complex operations like addition and subtraction, all while ensuring everyone gets a fair share of fruit?

Let Us Learn the Lesson

Funky Fruit Fractions: Using BODMAS at the Fruit Market!

Imagine you're at a vibrant fruit market overflowing with delicious treats!

But to get the perfect mix of fruits for your smoothie, you need to use your math skills, especially BODMAS, to handle those funky fractions!

B - Brackets (Grouping Fruits by Type):

- Brackets can represent groups of fruits you want to buy together.
- For example, if you need ½ watermelon and ¼ cantaloupe (both melons), you could group them in brackets: [(½ watermelon) + (¼ cantaloupe)].
- Remember, anything inside the brackets needs to be solved first!

O - Order of (Powers and Roots) (Not Used Here):

- This part of BODMAS doesn't apply to fruit shopping because we're not dealing with powers or roots (like square roots of apples!).

D - Division (Sharing Fruits):

- Division is crucial when you want to share a fruit with friends.
- You might divide the weight of a watermelon by the number of slices you want to get the weight of each slice.

M - Multiplication (Finding Total Fruit Amounts):

- Multiplication is your friend when buying multiple fruits of the same kind.
- You can multiply the price per fruit by the number of fruits to find the total cost.

A - Addition & S - Subtraction (Combining Fruits or Finding Differences):

- Addition helps you find the total weight of your fruits if you're buying a variety.
- You can add the weight of the watermelon, bananas, and grapes to find the total weight of your shopping basket.
- Subtraction can be handy if you change your mind and decide to take away some fruit before paying.

Making the Perfect Fruity Mixture with BODMAS:
Here's an example of how BODMAS helps you at the market:
[(½ watermelon) + (¼ cantaloupe)] / 2 + (1 ½ kg bananas) = Total fruit mix for smoothie
Following BODMAS:

1. Solve the bracketed section first: Find the total weight of the melons (½ watermelon + ¼ cantaloupe).
2. Then, divide the total melon weight by 2 (since you want half for your smoothie).
3. Finally, add the weight of the bananas to find the total weight of the fruit mix for your smoothie.

By understanding BODMAS, you can ensure you get the perfect amount of each fruit for your delicious and healthy smoothie!

Remember, BODMAS is a guide, and you might not use all the steps depending on your shopping choices. But with a little math magic, you'll be a whiz at navigating the fruit market in no time!

Check Your Basic Knowledge

1. **Banana Bonanza!** You want 1 ½ bananas for your smoothie and your friend wants ¾ of a banana. How much banana do you need in total? (Addition is used to find the total amount of banana)

2. **Melon Mania!** A watermelon weighs 5 kg. You want to use ½ of it for a fruit salad. How many kilograms of watermelon will you use? (Multiplication is used to find the weight of half the watermelon)

3. **Berry Balancing Act!** A bag of blueberries weighs ¼ kg and a bag of raspberries weighs ⅓ kg. How much heavier are the raspberries compared to the blueberries? (Subtraction is used to find the weight difference)

4. **Orange Order!** Oranges cost $0.50 each. You want to buy 3 oranges. How much will they cost in total? (Multiplication is used to find the total cost)

5. **Sharing Strawberries!** You have a container of strawberries and want to share them with 2 friends. There is enough for ½ cup each. How many cups of strawberries do you need in total? (Multiplication is used to find the total amount needed)

6. **Pineapple Puzzle!** A pineapple recipe requires ¼ cup of chopped pineapple. You have a whole pineapple that weighs 2 kg. If about ½ kg of a pineapple is usable, how much chopped pineapple will you get? (Multiplication is used to find the usable pineapple weight, then multiplication again to find the chopped amount)

7. **Grape Grouping!** A bunch of grapes weighs ½ kg. You need

¾ kg of grapes for a fruit platter. How much more weight do you need from another bunch? (Subtraction is used to find the remaining weight needed)

8. **Mango Mix-Up!** A recipe requires ½ cup of diced mango and ¼ cup of chopped banana. You accidentally used ¾ cup of banana. How much less diced mango do you need to add now? (Subtraction is used to find the remaining amount of mango needed after using extra banana)

9. **Apple Addition!** You buy ½ kg of apples and your friend brings another ¼ kg. How much apple do you have together for baking a pie? (Addition is used to find the total weight of apples)

10. **Watermelon Wonder!** You want to buy slices of watermelon. Each slice is ¼ of a whole watermelon, and a whole watermelon weighs 4 kg. How much does each slice weigh? (Division is used to find the weight of each slice)

Chapter 10: Cosmic Carnival Chaos!

The annual Cosmic Carnival had arrived, and the BODMAS Bunch were ecstatic!

It was a dazzling spectacle filled with whirling rides, neon lights, and games of chance (well, not exactly chance, with the BODMAS Bunch around!).

Captain Bracket, sporting a jaunty carnival hat, led the crew through the bustling crowds. Miss Addition's eyes sparkled brighter than the flashing lights, and Sergeant Times was already flexing his muscles, eager to win some giant stuffed space-whales.

Their first stop was the "Ring Toss Extravaganza." A friendly alien with three heads and six eyes greeted them. "Welcome, brave travelers! To win a prize, you must toss rings onto three poles. Each pole has a different number of points: 2, 4, and 5.

But there's a twist!

You need to solve a BODMAS equation first!"

He pointed towards a board with an equation: "(3 x 2) - 1 = ?"

Officer Of, his colon twitching with excitement, piped up. "Remember the order of operations, crew! Brackets come first!"

Working together, they solved the equation: 3 x 2 = 6, then subtracted 1, leaving them with 5 points. "We need to aim for the pole with 5 points!" declared Captain Bracket.

With a series of well-aimed throws, they managed to ring all three poles, scoring a perfect score and winning a giant, fluffy space-whale for Sergeant Times (who promptly used it as a giant pillow during the next game).

Their next challenge was the "Cosmic Calculator Coaster." This thrilling ride zipped and zagged through a series of screens displaying BODMAS problems. Riders had to answer correctly to keep the coaster on track!

The problems got trickier as the ride sped up, but the BODMAS Bunch used their teamwork and math skills to navigate the equations, keeping the coaster gliding smoothly and earning a shower of confetti at the end.

The day was filled with exciting games and challenges, all requiring a good grasp of BODMAS. They played "Balloon Blast," popping balloons with addition and subtraction problems written on them. They even tried their luck at the "Wacky Wheel," spinning a wheel with numbers and using BODMAS to determine their prize.

By the end of the day, the BODMAS Bunch had a backpack full of carnival goodies and a heart full of happy memories. They proved that math can be fun, especially at the Cosmic Carnival!

Activity: BODMAS Bonanza!

Calling all carnival champions!

Challenge yourselves with these fun and festive BODMAS worksheets filled with carnival-themed problems!

The worksheets can include a variety of problems involving:

- **Ring Toss:** Solve BODMAS equations to determine the

point value for each ring toss target.

- **Cosmic Coaster:** Answer BODMAS problems displayed on screens throughout the "coaster ride" to keep it moving forward.
- **Balloon Blast:** Pop balloons with addition and subtraction problems written on them. Each correct answer earns points!
- **Wacky Wheel:** Spin the wheel that has different numbers on each section. Use BODMAS to combine the number you landed on with another number displayed on the board to determine your prize.

Bonus Challenge: Can you create your own carnival game that uses BODMAS?

Design a game board, write fun BODMAS equations, and decide on prizes for correct answers!

Let Us Learn the Lesson

Cosmic Carnival Chaos: Conquering Challenges with BODMAS!

Welcome to the Cosmic Carnival, a mind-bending extravaganza where fun and games take on a whole new dimension!

But wait, there seems to be some chaos amidst the cosmic confetti. Don't worry, young space traveler, because BODMAS is here to save the day!

B - Brackets (Grouping Special Games):

- Imagine games with multiple parts or challenges. Brackets can represent these grouped activities.
- You might need to find the total points earned in a bracketed mini-game before moving on to the next challenge.
- Remember, anything inside the brackets needs to be solved first!

O - Order of (Powers and Roots) (Not Used Here):

- This part of BODMAS doesn't apply to the carnival because we're not dealing with powers or tricky space roots (like the square root of jumptastic jumps!).

D - Division (Sharing Prizes or Tickets):

- Division is crucial for sharing prizes or tickets fairly among carnival goers.
- You might divide the total number of tickets by the number of players to find how many each gets.

M - Multiplication (Calculating Points or Scores):

- Multiplication comes in handy when games involve collecting points or completing tasks with a point value.
- You can multiply the number of tasks completed by the points per task to find the total score.

A - Addition & S - Subtraction (Combining Scores or Finding Differences):

- Addition helps you find your total score if you participate in multiple games throughout the carnival.
- You can add the points from each game to see your grand total.
- Subtraction can be useful if you need to figure out how many more tickets you need to buy a special prize after spending some.

Solving Cosmic Chaos with BODMAS:

Here's an example of how BODMAS helps you navigate the carnival:

(Points from ring toss game) x 2 + [(Tickets won from spaceship race) / 3] = Total points and tickets earned

Following BODMAS:

1. Solve the bracketed section first: Divide the total tickets won in the race by 3 to find how many each person gets.
2. Then, multiply the points from the ring toss game by 2 (if it was a double-points round).
3. Finally, add the points from the ring toss game to the number of tickets you received to find your total earnings.

By following BODMAS, you can ensure you score high, win amazing prizes, and conquer the cosmic chaos of the carnival!

Remember, BODMAS is a guide, and the specific challenges you encounter might not use all the steps. But with a good grasp of these concepts, you'll be a champion carnival goer in no time!

Check Your Basic Knowledge

1. **Rocket Race Ruckus!** The rocket race awards 10 points per lap. If you complete 3 laps, how many points do you earn? (Multiplication is used to find the total points)
2. **Wacky Weightlessness!** The anti-gravity game awards points based on time spent floating. You float for 20 seconds and your friend floats for 15 seconds. The game awards 5 points per second. How many points do you earn together? (Addition is used to find the total time floating, then multiplication to find total points)
3. **Cosmic Quiz Conundrum!** A correct answer in the quiz is worth 3 points, and an incorrect answer deducts 1 point. You answer 5 questions correctly and 2 incorrectly. What is your total score? (Multiplication is used to find points for correct answers, then subtraction to find the final score)
4. **Alien Art Extravaganza!** The painting competition awards

double points for using sparkly space dust. You get 10 points normally, but used space dust. How many points do you win? (Multiplication is used to find the total points with the bonus)

5. **Zero-Gravity Games Galore!** You win 15 tickets playing Zero-G hoops and your friend wins 10 tickets playing Lunar Leap. How many tickets do you have together for some cosmic candy? (Addition is used to find the total number of tickets)

6. **Intergalactic Treasure Hunt!** The treasure hunt has 3 clues, each worth 5 points for solving them correctly. How many points do you earn by completing the entire hunt? (Multiplication is used to find the total points for all clues)

7. **Bumper Rocket Race Ruckus!** The bumper rocket race awards 8 points per win. You win 2 races. How many points do you earn in total? (Multiplication is used to find the total points for winning races)

8. **Cosmic Cafe Challenge!** A spaceship ice cream costs 12 tickets. You have 20 tickets. After buying the ice cream, how many tickets do you have left? (Subtraction is used to find the remaining tickets)

9. **Interplanetary Photo Booth!** A photo with a friendly Martian costs 5 tickets and a photo with a dancing robot costs 3 tickets. How much will it cost for both photos? (Addition is used to find the total ticket cost)

10. **Souvenir Scramble!** You need 25 tickets for a cool space badge. You win 10 tickets playing Astro-Bowling. How many more tickets do you need to buy the badge? (Subtraction is used to find the remaining tickets needed)

Chapter 11: Monster Mash Up!

On a spooky night with a full moon glowing overhead, the BODMAS Bunch received an invitation to a very special party - a Monster Mash Up!

They were thrilled to be attending a gathering of friendly monsters who loved nothing more than spooky snacks, spooky games, and, of course, spooky potions!

Miss Addition, ever the helpful one, volunteered to bring a batch of her famous "Bubbling Brain Booster" potion. But there was a problem. Her recipe book was filled with mysterious symbols and cryptic messages.

"Don't worry, Miss Addition," boomed Sergeant Times, his voice echoing in the dimly lit room. "We can use BODMAS to decipher the recipe!"

Captain Bracket, ever the leader, chimed in. "That's a great idea, Sergeant! Remember, BODMAS helps us follow the correct order when mixing ingredients."

The recipe for the "Bubbling Brain Booster" looked like this:

Ingredients:

- Bat Wings (B) - 2
- Glowworm Goo (G) - (3 x 2)
- Eyeball Extract (E) - 4
- Swamp Water (S) - B + G - E

Officer Of, his colon flashing with concentration, squinted at the recipe. "We need to follow BODMAS step by step!" he declared.

First, they tackled the part inside the brackets for the Glowworm Goo: 3 x 2 = 6. This meant they needed 6 scoops of Glowworm Goo.

Next, they focused on the Swamp Water. Miss Addition, her eyes gleaming with excitement, pointed out that addition and subtraction come after multiplication and division. So, they needed to add the Bat Wings (2) and the Glowworm Goo (6) first, giving them a total of 8. Then, they would subtract the Eyeball Extract (4), leaving them with a final amount of 4 scoops of Swamp Water.

With a series of careful measurements and a sprinkle of BODMAS magic, Miss Addition concocted a perfect batch of "Bubbling Brain Booster" potion, sure to make the monsters' brains extra sharp for the party games.

At the Monster Mash Up, Miss Addition's potion was a huge hit!

The monsters loved the brain-boosting effects, allowing them to win all the spooky trivia games and even come up with hilarious monster puns.

The night was filled with laughter, spooky snacks, and a newfound appreciation for BODMAS, proving that even monsters can benefit from a little math magic!

Activity: The Monster Mash Up Mixology Lab!

Calling all junior monster mixologists!

Let's create some spooky potions for the next Monster Mash Up party!

What you'll need:

- Construction paper in various colors
- Markers
- Scissors
- Glue stick
- Plastic cups or bowls (to represent cauldrons)
- Spoons (for stirring)

How to play:

1. **Design your potion labels:** On construction paper, create labels for your spooky potions with fun names like "Bubbling Brain Booster" or "Giggle Gargoyle Goo."
2. **Write your BODMAS recipes:** Below the potion name, write the recipe using fun ingredients like "Bat Tears" (BT), "Spider Silk" (SS), "Toadstool Powder" (TP), etc. Use addition, subtraction, multiplication, and division to create the recipe, incorporating BODMAS order.
3. **Mix and match:** Let your friends or family choose a potion recipe and use toy ingredients (beans, cereal pieces, etc.) to "mix" the potion according to the BODMAS instructions written on the label.

Bonus Challenge: Can you create your own spooky potion with a secret ingredient that requires solving a BODMAS equation to reveal its quantity?

Let Us Learn the Lesson

Monster Mash Up: Using BODMAS to Survive a Spooky Spooktacular!

Get ready for a monstrously fun night at the Halloween carnival! But beware, there might be some spooky challenges and costume conundrums along the way.

No worries though, because BODMAS is your secret weapon to navigate the monster mash up!

B - Brackets (Grouping Costumes or Treats):

- Imagine a costume contest with multiple categories (e.g., scariest, funniest). Brackets can represent these categories.
- You might need to find the total number of points awarded in a bracketed category before comparing it to other categories.
- Remember, anything inside the brackets needs to be solved first!

O - Order of (Powers and Roots) (Not Used Here):

- This part of BODMAS doesn't apply to the monster mash because we're not dealing with superpowers or spooky square roots (like the square root of ghosts!).

D - Division (Sharing Candy or Points):

- Division is crucial when sharing candy with your friends or dividing points among winners in a game.
- You might divide the total number of lollipops by the number of trick-or-treaters to ensure everyone gets a fair share.

M - Multiplication (Calculating Scores or Candy Count):

- Multiplication comes in handy when games involve collecting points or candy with point values.
- You can multiply the number of correct answers in a monster

quiz by the points per answer to find your total score.

A - Addition & S - Subtraction (Combining Scores or Finding Differences):

- Addition helps you find your total candy collection after a night of trick-or-treating.
- You can add the candy from each house you visit to see your grand total.
- Subtraction can be useful if you want to figure out how much candy you have left after sharing some with your friends.

Conquering the Monster Mash Up with BODMAS:

Here's an example of how BODMAS helps you survive the spooky fun:

(Points from mummy wrapping contest) x 3 + [(Candy collected from 5 houses) / 2] = Total score and candy

Following BODMAS:

1. Solve the bracketed section first: Divide the total candy collected by 2 (if you're sharing half with a friend).
2. Then, multiply the points from the mummy wrapping contest by 3 (if it was a triple-point round).
3. Finally, add the points from the contest to the number of candies you kept to find your total score (points + candy).

By following BODMAS, you can ensure you have a fang-tastic time, win spooky prizes, and navigate the monster mash up like a champ!

Remember, BODMAS is a guide, and the specific challenges you encounter might not use all the steps. But with a good understanding of these concepts, you'll be a master monster masher in no time!

Check Your Basic Knowledge

1. **Creepy Cookie Contest!** The cookie decorating contest awards 5 points for creativity and 3 points for spookiness. Your cookie gets 5 points for creativity. If double points are awarded for most spiderwebs (which yours has!), how many points do you earn in total? (Multiplication is used to find the total points with the bonus)

2. **Pumpkin Bowling Bonanza!** You knock down 7 pins in pumpkin bowling. Each pin is worth 2 points. How many points do you score? (Multiplication is used to find the total points)

3. **Ghost Guessing Game!** You guess 3 ghosts correctly in the game (each worth 4 points) and miss 1 (which deducts 2 points). What is your total score? (Multiplication is used to find points for correct guesses, then subtraction to find the final score)

4. **Monster Mash Dance-Off!** You win 1st place in the dance-off, which awards 10 points. 2nd place gets 8 points and 3rd place gets 6 points. How many total points are awarded for the top 3 places? (Addition is used to find the total points for all placements)

5. **Sharing Scary Stories!** You have 12 lollipops and your friend has 8. How many lollipops do you have together to share with other monsters? (Addition is used to find the total number of lollipops)

6. **Costume Catastrophe!** Your monster costume needs 3 fake eyeballs. A bag of eyeballs has 10. After using what you need, how many eyeballs are left in the bag? (Subtraction is used to find the remaining eyeballs)

7. **Haunted House Hustle!** The haunted house charges 5 tickets per person. You and 2 friends go in. How many tickets do you need in total? (Multiplication is used to find the total cost for your group)

8. **Witching Potion Challenge!** The potion-making contest awards points based on the number of ingredients used (each worth 1 point). You use 8 ingredients. How many points do you earn? (Multiplication is used to find the total points for all ingredients)

9. **Bobbing for Apples Extravaganza!** You bob for 4 apples and your friend bobs for 3. How many apples do you have together for a spooky snack? (Addition is used to find the total number of apples)

10. **Monster Mash Up Mayhem!** You win 15 tickets playing Monster Mini-Golf. A spooky mask costs 10 tickets. After buying the mask, how many tickets do you have left? (Subtraction is used to find the remaining tickets)

Chapter 12: Robot Repair Roundup!

In the bustling metropolis of Megacity 1000, the BODMAS Bunch were enjoying a well-deserved vacation. But their relaxation was short-lived when a frantic signal blared from their robotic friend, Bolts.

"Help! Help!" Bolts' metallic voice crackled through their communicator. "There's been a power surge, and all my circuits are fried!

I can't move and I can't think straight!"

Without hesitation, the BODMAS Bunch sprang into action. They zoomed towards Bolts' repair bay, their spaceship landing with a soft thud.

"Don't worry, Bolts," soothed Captain Bracket. "We'll get you back online in no time. But this repair job will require all our BODMAS expertise!"

Miss Addition, ever the problem-solver, chimed in. "It seems the power surge scrambled the instructions for your repair modules. We need to solve the BODMAS equations to figure out which parts need fixing first!"

Sergeant Times, his muscles rippling with determination, scanned Bolts' deactivated form. "Looks like his circuits are fried! Let's get to work!"

Bolts' repair manual was projected onto a holographic screen. It displayed a scrambled mess of numbers, symbols, and robot parts.

The first equation they encountered was:

$8 + (2 \times 3) = ?$

Officer Of, his colon flashing with concentration, piped up. "Remember the order of operations! Brackets come first!"

Working together, they solved the equation: $2 \times 3 = 6$, then added 8, giving them a final answer of 14.

Following the manual's instructions, they realized 14 corresponded to the "Central Logic Unit." With a series of careful maneuvers and a few solved BODMAS equations later, they managed to replace the fried unit and reboot Bolts' central systems.

The next equation involved replacing a faulty "Energy Core." The equation read:

$(5 \times 4) - 3 = ?$

Following BODMAS, they multiplied 5×4 first, resulting in 20. Then, they subtracted 3, giving them a final answer of 17.

By solving more BODMAS equations, they replaced faulty wires, repaired dented panels, and recalibrated Bolts' internal sensors. Finally, with a triumphant whir and a flash of blue light, Bolts came back online!

"I'm operational again!" boomed Bolts, his voice strong and clear. "Thanks to you, the BODMAS Bunch, I'm back in action!"

The rest of the day was spent catching up and enjoying Bolts' witty robot humor. The experience once again proved that BODMAS wasn't just for schoolwork - it was a valuable skill that could even help fix a friend in need!

Activity: Reassemble Robo 5000!

Calling all junior robot mechanics!

It's your turn to use BODMAS to bring Robo 5000 back to life!

What you'll need:

- Worksheet with a large picture of a disassembled robot (Robo 5000)
- The robot will be missing various parts (head, arms, legs, etc.)
- Beside each missing part will be a BODMAS equation.

How to play:

1. Solve each BODMAS equation on the worksheet.
2. The answer to each equation will correspond to a specific robot part (e.g., the answer to 3 + 2 might correspond to the robot's left arm).
3. Once you've solved all the equations and identified the corresponding parts, use crayons or markers to "reassemble" Robo 5000 on the worksheet!

Bonus Challenge: Can you create your own robot with missing parts?

Write BODMAS equations that correspond to each missing part, and challenge your friends or family to solve the equations to complete your robot design!

Let Us Learn the Lesson

Robot Repair Roundup: Using BODMAS to Fix the Funfair Droids!

The funfair robots are malfunctioning, and it's up to you, the tech whiz, to get them back in action!

But to diagnose the problems and fix the circuits, you'll need your brainpower and a handy tool called BODMAS.

B - Brackets (Grouping Faulty Circuits):

- Imagine a robot with multiple malfunctioning circuits. Brackets can represent these grouped circuits that need to be fixed together.
- You might need to find the total time it takes to repair the bracketed circuits before moving on to other parts of the robot.
- Remember, anything inside the brackets needs to be solved first!

O - Order of (Powers and Roots) (Not Used Here):

- This part of BODMAS doesn't apply to robot repair because we're not dealing with electrical powers or wires with square roots (we hope!).

D - Division (Sharing Spare Parts or Tools):

- Division is crucial when you need to share spare parts or tools efficiently among multiple robots that need fixing.
- You might divide the total number of wrenches by the number of repair stations to ensure each station has enough tools.

M - Multiplication (Calculating Repair Time or Parts Needed):

- Multiplication comes in handy when estimating the repair time or the number of parts needed based on the complexity of the problem.
- You can multiply the number of malfunctioning circuits by the average repair time per circuit to find the total repair time for a group of circuits.

A - Addition & S - Subtraction (Combining Parts or Finding Differences):

- Addition helps you find the total number of parts you need to fix all the robots if there are multiple types of parts needed.
- You can add the number of new wires needed for one robot to the number of chips needed for another to find the total parts required.
- Subtraction can be useful if you need to figure out how many spare parts you have left after fixing a robot.

Fixing the Funfair with BODMAS:

Here's an example of how BODMAS helps you become a robot repair champion:

(Repair time for circuits in [arm]) + (Repair time for circuits in [sensor panel]) x 2 = Total repair time

Following BODMAS:

1. Solve the bracketed sections first: Find the repair time for each set of circuits (arm and sensor panel).
2. Then, multiply the repair time for the sensor panel by 2 (if it's a more complex repair).
3. Finally, add the repair times for both sections to find the total time to fix the robot.

By following BODMAS, you can diagnose problems efficiently, fix the robots quickly, and get the funfair back up and running in no time!

Remember, BODMAS is a guide, and the specific repairs you encounter might not use all the steps. But with a good grasp of these concepts, you'll be a whiz at robot repair roundups!

Check Your Basic Knowledge

1. **Rusty Rivet Repair!** It takes 10 minutes to fix a loose screw and 5 minutes to replace a burnt-out light bulb. How long will it take to fix both if done one after the other? (Addition is used to find the total repair time)

2. **Broken Bolt Blues!** One robot arm needs 2 new bolts. Another robot leg needs 4 new bolts. How many bolts do you need in total? (Addition is used to find the total number of bolts needed)

3. **Power Pack Puzzle!** A robot needs 3 AA batteries and another robot needs 2 AA batteries. If you have a pack of 8 batteries, how many batteries are left after replacing the ones in the robots? (Subtraction is used to find the remaining batteries)

4. **Spare Parts Sharing!** You have 6 screwdrivers and your friend brings 4 screwdrivers to help with repairs. How many screwdrivers do you have together to fix the robots? (Addition is used to find the total number of screwdrivers)

5. **Sensor Sizzle!** It takes 15 minutes to repair one faulty sensor. Two robots each have a malfunctioning sensor. How long will it take to fix the sensors in both robots? (Multiplication is used to find the total repair time)

6. **Gear Glitch Gremlin!** Each robot leg needs 3 gears to be replaced. If one robot has 2 malfunctioning legs, how many gears do you need in total? (Multiplication is used to find the total number of gears needed)

7. **Wrench Round-Up!** There are 3 repair stations and you have 12 wrenches. If you want to distribute the wrenches equally, how many wrenches will each station have? (Division is used to find the number of wrenches per station)

8. **Capacitor Catastrophe!** One robot needs a new capacitor, which takes 20 minutes to install. Another robot needs a software update, which takes 10 minutes. How much longer does the capacitor replacement take compared to the software update? (Subtraction is used to find the time difference)

9. **Microchip Mishap!** A robot needs 4 microchips to function properly. You have a box with 10 microchips. After fixing the

robot, how many microchips are left in the box? (Subtraction is used to find the remaining microchips)

10. **Double Doohickey Dilemma!** A doohickey (a special robot part) takes 8 minutes to fix. Two robots each have a broken doohickey. How long will it take to fix the doohickeys in both robots? (Multiplication is used to find the total repair time)

Chapter 13: Space Race Surprise!

The annual Intergalactic Space Race was upon them, and the BODMAS Bunch were buzzing with excitement. This year, Captain Bracket had entered their trusty spaceship, the "Equationator," into the competition. They were up against a motley crew of space racers, each with their own unique starship.

The racecourse was a dazzling spectacle, a swirling nebula filled with twinkling stars and cosmic dust. But this wasn't your ordinary race. At various checkpoints scattered throughout the nebula, the racers would encounter challenges - challenges that required BODMAS mastery!

"First checkpoint approaching!" boomed Officer Of, his colon flashing with anticipation.

A holographic screen flickered to life, displaying an equation:

$4 \times (2 + 1) = ?$

Miss Addition practically vibrated with excitement. "Remember BODMAS, crew! Brackets come first!" she chirped.

Working together, they solved the equation: 2 + 1 = 3, then multiplied 4 x 3, giving them a final answer of 12.

"Correct answer!" boomed a voice from the screen. "The Equationator may proceed!"

With a surge of power, the Equationator blasted past the checkpoint, leaving a trail of glittering stardust behind.

The next checkpoint presented a trickier equation:

$(8 / 2) + 3 = ?$

Corporal Division, his diagonal slash symbol gleaming, took charge. "Division comes first, Captain!" he declared.

Following BODMAS, they divided 8 by 2, resulting in 4. Then, they added 3, giving them a final answer of 7.

As they conquered each checkpoint, solving BODMAS equations with increasing difficulty, the other racers started to fall behind. Some struggled with complex multiplication problems, while others got tripped up by the order of operations.

Finally, after a thrilling race through the nebula, the Equationator emerged victorious! The BODMAS Bunch erupted in cheers, their spaceship bathed in the golden glow of the winner's podium.

"We knew our BODMAS skills would come in handy!" beamed Miss Addition.

Sergeant Times, ever the show-off, puffed out his chest. "Easy as pie... well, almost as easy!"

Captain Bracket, his smile as bright as a supernova, addressed the crowd. "This victory proves that knowledge is power, even in the vastness of space. And remember, a little BODMAS can take you a long way!"

Activity: The BODMAS Blast Off Board Game!

Calling all aspiring space racers!

Get ready to blast off on an intergalactic adventure with the BODMAS Bunch in this exciting board game!

What you'll need:

- Game board decorated with a space race theme, featuring checkpoints with BODMAS equations.
- Spaceship tokens for each player (you can use buttons, coins, or small toy spaceships).
- Dice (one or two, depending on the game mechanics you choose).
- Small markers to keep track of each player's position on the board.

How to play:

1. Players take turns rolling the dice and moving their spaceship tokens along the game board.
2. Landing on a checkpoint space requires the player to solve the BODMAS equation displayed on that space.
3. If the player solves the equation correctly, they can move ahead a designated number of spaces.
4. If the player solves the equation incorrectly, they might lose a turn or have to move back a few spaces.
5. The first player to reach the finish line wins the game and is crowned the ultimate BODMAS Blast Off Champion!

Bonus Challenge: Can you create your own BODMAS equations for the checkpoint spaces on the game board?

You can also design special spaces with unique challenges that involve BODMAS and movement on the board.

Let Us Learn the Lesson

Space Race Surprise: Conquering Challenges with BODMAS on a Stellar Mission!

Get ready for a thrilling adventure as you blast off on a space race!

But buckle up, young astronaut, because there might be unexpected challenges and cosmic calculations along the way. No worries though, because BODMAS is your secret weapon to navigate the space race surprise!

B - Brackets (Grouping Tasks or Fuel Needs):

- Imagine a mission with multiple tasks or objectives. Brackets can represent these grouped activities.
- You might need to find the total amount of fuel needed for the bracketed tasks before moving on to the next part of the mission.
- Remember, anything inside the brackets needs to be solved first!

O - Order of (Powers and Roots) (Not Used Here):

- This part of BODMAS doesn't apply to space travel because we're not dealing with rocket superpowers or the square root of distant galaxies (at least, not yet!).

D - Division (Sharing Supplies or Resources):

- Division is crucial when you need to share food supplies or other resources fairly among your crewmates on the spaceship.
- You might divide the total amount of space pizza by the number of astronauts to ensure everyone gets a slice.

M - Multiplication (Calculating Distances or Time):

- Multiplication comes in handy when calculating travel distances or time between planets.
- You can multiply the speed of your spaceship by the distance

to a planet to find the total travel time.

A - Addition & S - Subtraction (Combining Supplies or Finding Differences):

- Addition helps you find the total amount of fuel you have left after completing a mission if you started with a certain amount and used some during the journey.
- You can add the fuel used for one part of the mission to the fuel used for another part to find the total used.
- Subtraction can be useful if you need to figure out how much farther you can travel with the remaining fuel after a course correction.

Winning the Space Race with BODMAS:

Here's an example of how BODMAS helps you win the space race:

(Fuel used for [orbiting the Moon]) + (Distance to Mars / Speed of spaceship) = Total fuel used and travel time

Following BODMAS:

1. Solve the bracketed section first: Find the amount of fuel used for orbiting the Moon.
2. Then, divide the distance to Mars by the speed of your spaceship to find the travel time.
3. Finally, add the fuel used for orbiting the Moon to the travel time to Mars to find the total fuel used and estimated travel time.

By following BODMAS, you can ensure your spaceship runs smoothly, manage resources efficiently, and become a champion space racer!

Remember, BODMAS is a guide, and the specific challenges you encounter might not use all the steps. But with a good understanding of these concepts, you'll be a master of any space race surprise!

Check Your Basic Knowledge

1. **Cosmic Calibration Challenge!** Your spaceship needs 10 units of fuel to reach the space station and another 5 units to land there. How much fuel do you need in total for the entire journey? (Addition is used to find the total fuel needed)

2. **Alien Appetizer Adventure!** You have 12 space cookies for the trip and share them equally with your 2 astronaut friends. How many cookies does each astronaut get? (Division is used to find the number of cookies per person)

3. **Moon Mission Mania!** It takes 2 hours to travel around the Moon and 1 hour to land on the lunar surface. How much total time will you spend on the Moon? (Addition is used to find the total time spent on the Moon)

4. **Orbiting Obstacle Course!** If you need to travel around Mars 5 times to complete your mission, and each orbit takes 30 minutes, how long will it take in total? (Multiplication is used to find the total travel time)

5. **Fuel Tank Fun!** Your spaceship starts with 80 units of fuel. After traveling for a bit, you use 10 units. How much fuel do you have remaining? (Subtraction is used to find the remaining fuel)

6. **Meteorite Munchies!** There are 6 energy bars for the crew and you buy another 4 at a spaceport. How many energy bars do you have total for the journey? (Addition is used to find the total number of energy bars)

7. **Water Tank Woes!** The water tank holds 50 liters of water. Your crew uses 15 liters during the first part of the space race. How much water is left in the tank? (Subtraction is used to find the remaining water)

8. **Spaceship Speed Challenge!** Your spaceship travels at 500 kilometers per hour. If the planet X-22 is 2000 kilometers

away, how long will it take to get there? (Division is used to find the travel time)

9. **Packing for Pluto!** You pack 3 astronaut suits and your friend packs 2. How many suits do you have together for the mission to Pluto? (Addition is used to find the total number of suits)

10. **Cosmic Communication Conundrum!** It takes a signal 20 minutes to reach Earth from Mars. You send 2 messages back home. How long will it take to receive both messages? (Multiplication is used to find the total time to receive messages)

Chapter 14: Mystery on the Moon Base!

Alarm sirens blared throughout Lunar Base One, shattering the peaceful silence of the moon colony. Captain Bracket, ever the calm leader, sprang into action. "There's been a malfunction in the Anti-Gravity Chamber!" he declared.

Rushing to the control room, they found Miss Addition slumped over a console, her face pale with worry. "The controls are locked down!" she exclaimed. "A series of cryptic messages appeared on the screen, and I can't decipher them!"

Sergeant Times, his muscles twitching with determination, peered at the screen. The messages were a jumbled mess of numbers, symbols, and lunar coordinates.

"It looks like a code!" boomed Officer Of, his colon flashing with concentration. "Maybe it involves BODMAS?"

With a glimmer of hope, they decided to analyze the messages. The first one read:

$$2 \times (3 + 1) = N$$

Corporal Division, his diagonal slash symbol gleaming, pointed out the variable N. "This could be the first coordinate!" he declared.

Following BODMAS, they solved the equation: $2 \times 4 = 8$. So, N likely represented the number 8.

The next message was even trickier:

$$(5 / 2) + 4 = E$$

Miss Addition, her eyes regaining their spark, took charge. "Division first!" she announced. They divided 5 by 2, resulting in 2.5. However, coordinates likely dealt with whole numbers. Rounding 2.5 up to 3, they added 4, giving them a possible value of 7 for E.

Following this pattern, they deciphered more messages, each one involving a BODMAS equation and a corresponding variable representing a moon base coordinate. With each solved equation, they inched closer to the source of the malfunction.

Finally, after a series of calculations and a thrilling maze-like journey through the moon base corridors (avoiding malfunctioning robots and flickering lights!), they arrived at the designated coordinates.

There, they found a malfunctioning power converter, its circuits overloaded. Using their engineering skills and a sprinkle of BODMAS magic, they managed to fix the converter and restore the Anti-Gravity Chamber's functionality.

Back in the control room, Miss Addition sighed with relief as the Anti-Gravity Chamber whirred back to life. "Thanks to your BODMAS expertise, crew, we averted a major disaster!"

Sergeant Times, ever the jokester, flexed his muscles. "Just another day at the office for the BODMAS Bunch!"

The mystery of the moon base was solved, proving that even in the lunar expanse, a sharp mind and a good grasp of BODMAS could save the day.

Activity: Lunar Labyrinth!

Calling all junior moon explorers!

Help the BODMAS Bunch navigate the Lunar Labyrinth to reach the malfunctioning power converter and restore gravity control!

What you'll need:

- Large sheet of construction paper decorated as a moon base maze.
- The maze path should have checkpoints marked with BODMAS equations.
- Small game piece to represent the player (astronaut figure, spaceship token, etc.)
- Pencil

How to play:

1. Start at the entrance of the Lunar Labyrinth maze.
2. As you reach each checkpoint, solve the BODMAS equation written there.
3. The answer to the equation will tell you which direction to take in the maze (e.g., answer is 2, so move two spaces to the right).
4. Continue solving equations and navigating the maze until you reach the designated location of the malfunctioning power converter (marked with a special symbol on the maze).
5. Congratulations! You've helped the BODMAS Bunch restore gravity control on the moon base!

Bonus Challenge: Can you create your own BODMAS maze with a different theme (forest, underwater, etc.)?

Design the maze paths and incorporate BODMAS equations at checkpoints to guide players through the maze to reach a specific destination.

Let Us Learn the Lesson

Mystery on the Moon Base: Cracking the Case with BODMAS!
Alert!
There's been a mysterious power outage on the moon base!
Don't panic, lunar detective!
With your keen mind and a dash of BODMAS, you'll solve the case and get the power back online.

B - Brackets (Grouping Power Cells):

- Imagine the moon base has multiple sections with separate power cells. Brackets can represent these grouped power cells.
- You might need to find the total amount of energy each section uses before comparing it to the overall power supply.
- Remember, anything inside the brackets needs to be solved first!

O - Order of (Powers and Roots) (Not Used Here):

- This part of BODMAS isn't relevant to this lunar whodunit because we're not dealing with supervillain powers or the square root of missing moon rocks (hopefully!).

D - Division (Sharing Power or Analyzing Data):

- Division is crucial when figuring out how much power to distribute to different areas of the moon base.
- You might divide the total power output by the number of operational labs to see if each lab is receiving enough energy.

M - Multiplication (Calculating Energy Use or Time):

- Multiplication comes in handy when estimating energy consumption or how long backup power can last.
- You can multiply the number of active machines in a section by the power usage per machine to find the total energy used.

A - Addition & S - Subtraction (Combining Power Needs or Finding Differences):

- Addition helps you find the total energy used by the entire moon base if you have data from each section.
- You can add the energy used in the living quarters to the energy used in the labs to find the base's total consumption.
- Subtraction can be useful if you need to figure out how much extra power is needed after accounting for current usage.

Solving the Lunar Mystery with BODMAS:

Here's an example of how BODMAS helps you crack the case:

(Energy used in labs + Energy used in living quarters) - Available power = Missing power source

Following BODMAS:

1. Solve the bracketed section first: Find the total energy used by adding the energy used in each section.
2. Then, subtract the available power from the total energy used to find the amount of missing power.
3. This difference might point you to a faulty power cell or an overloaded system.

By following BODMAS, you can analyze power consumption patterns, identify the culprit behind the outage, and become a hero of the moon base!

Remember, BODMAS is a guide, and the specific steps you take might vary depending on the clues you find.

But with a good grasp of these concepts, you'll be a whiz at solving mysteries on the moon base!

Check Your Basic Knowledge

1. **Solar Panel Surprise!** One section of the moon base uses 10

units of power and another section uses 15 units. How much power do they use together? (Addition is used to find the total power usage)

2. **Rover Repair Request!** A rover uses 5 units of power per hour. If it needs to be repaired for 3 hours, how much power will it use in total? (Multiplication is used to find the total power used)

3. **Oxygenator Overload?** The oxygenator uses 20 units of power and the living quarters use 12 units. The total power available is 40 units. Is there enough power for both right now? (Subtraction is used to find the remaining power after powering the oxygenator)

4. **Greenhouse Gremlins!** The greenhouse uses 8 units of power and the control room uses 6 units. How much more power does the greenhouse use compared to the control room? (Subtraction is used to find the power difference)

5. **Backup Battery Boost!** The backup battery has 50 units of power. If 10 units are used during the outage, how much power remains? (Subtraction is used to find the remaining power)

6. **Lab Light Left On!** Each lab light uses 2 units of power. If 3 lights are left on in one lab, how much power are they using together? (Multiplication is used to find the total power used by the lights)

7. **Power Cell Pu puzzler!** The hydroponics lab uses 15 units of power and the communication center uses 8 units. If they are on separate power cells, how much total power is being used by both labs? (Addition is used to find the total power used)

8. **Moon Buggy Mishap!** The moon buggy uses 7 units of power per hour. If it gets stuck and needs to run for an extra 2 hours, how much additional power will it use? (Multiplication is used to find the extra power used)

9. **Climate Control Conundrum!** The climate control system uses 25 units of power per hour. If it needs to run for 4 hours to regulate the moon base temperature, how much power will it use in total? (Multiplication is used to find the total power used)

10. **Power Consumption Challenge!** The research lab uses 12 units of power and the medical bay uses 10 units. Together, how much power do these two important areas use? (Addition is used to find the total power used)

Chapter 15: BODMAS Olympics!

The excitement crackled in the air as the BODMAS Bunch arrived at the majestic Colosseum Mathematicus, the venue for the prestigious BODMAS Olympics!

Teams from all corners of the mathematical universe had gathered to compete in a series of mind-bending challenges, all centered around the power of BODMAS.

Captain Bracket, his competitive spirit ignited, rallied the crew. "Alright, BODMAS Bunch! Let's show them what we're made of!"

The Olympics kicked off with a thrilling relay race. Each team member had to solve a BODMAS equation at their designated station, passing a baton (or in this case, a giant abacus!) to the next teammate only after getting the correct answer. Miss Addition, with her lightning-fast calculations, was a blur at her station. Sergeant Times, determined not to be outdone, tackled his division problem with impressive speed.

The next challenge was the "Cosmic Calculator Caper." Teams were presented with a series of cryptic messages displayed on giant holographic screens. These messages involved hidden codes that, when deciphered using BODMAS, revealed the location of hidden mathematical treasures scattered throughout the Colosseum Mathematicus. Officer Of, his colon flashing with concentration, led the charge, his keen eye spotting patterns and hidden clues within the equations.

The final challenge was the ultimate test of BODMAS mastery - the "Mastermind Maze." Teams had to navigate a complex maze filled with tricky BODMAS equations at each turn. Solving the equation correctly allowed them to proceed, while a wrong answer sent them back a few spaces. Corporal Division, his diagonal slash symbol practically glowing, used his strategic thinking to guide the BODMAS Bunch through the maze's twists and turns.

After a day of intense competition and a healthy dose of friendly rivalry, the BODMAS Bunch emerged victorious!

They stood proudly on the podium, medals gleaming around their necks, a testament to their BODMAS prowess.

But for the BODMAS Bunch, it wasn't just about winning. It was about celebrating the joy of math, the power of teamwork, and the importance of BODMAS in solving problems, big or small.

Activity: The BODMAS Bunch Challenge!

Calling all future math champions!

Are you ready to put your BODMAS skills to the test?

Then join the BODMAS Bunch Challenge!

What you'll need:

- Worksheet filled with a variety of BODMAS problems, incorporating the different challenges from the story (e.g., relay race problems, code-deciphering problems, maze problems).

- Pen or pencil
- Timer (optional, for timed challenges)

How to play:

1. Work through the various BODMAS problems on the worksheet, either individually or in teams (like a mini-Olympics!).
2. Some problems might involve time pressure, so you can use a timer to add an extra layer of challenge (optional).
3. Check your answers and celebrate your successes!

Bonus Challenge: Can you create your own BODMAS challenge inspired by the story?

This could be a new event for the BODMAS Olympics or a fun activity for your friends and family. Design the challenge, write BODMAS problems, and test your skills (and theirs!)

Let Us Learn the Lesson

BODMAS Olympics: A Fun and Competitive Way to Master Order of Operations!

Get ready for some friendly competition in the BODMAS Olympics!

Here, athletes (that's you and your classmates!) will compete in various challenges that test their skills in using BODMAS (or PEMDAS in some countries) – the order of operations in math.

BODMAS stands for:

- **B**rackets (grouping)
- **O**rder of powers and roots (not used in this version)
- **D**ivision
- **M**ultiplication
- **A**ddition
- **S**ubtraction

The "Olympics" theme adds a fun twist to learning BODMAS. Each event will focus on a specific part of BODMAS, allowing you to practice and master each concept in a competitive yet enjoyable way.

Here's how the BODMAS Olympics might work:

- **Warm-Up Round: Brackets Bonanza!**
  - Athletes are given problems that involve calculations within brackets. They need to solve what's inside the brackets first before proceeding with the rest of the equation.
- **Multiplication Marathon:**
  - This event focuses on problems involving multiplication. Athletes compete to solve equations with the most multiplications in the shortest time.
- **Division Dash:**
  - This event focuses on division problems. Athletes race to find the correct answers, demonstrating their understanding of division.
- **Addition & Subtraction Relay:**
  - Here, athletes work in teams, taking turns solving problems involving addition and subtraction. The first team to finish the relay race with all answers correct wins.
- **The BODMAS Decathlon:**
  - The ultimate test! This event combines all aspects of BODMAS. Athletes solve complex equations that involve multiple operations, needing to follow the correct order.

Remember:

- BODMAS acts like the "rules" of the competition. Following them ensures accurate solutions and helps you become a

BODMAS champion!

Benefits of BODMAS Olympics:

- Makes learning BODMAS more engaging and interactive.
- Provides a competitive yet fun way to practice math skills.
- Encourages teamwork and problem-solving abilities.

So, grab your calculators (optional!), put on your thinking caps, and get ready to compete in the exciting world of BODMAS Olympics!

Check Your Basic Knowledge

BODMAS Olympics Practice Problems:

Welcome to the fun and challenging BODMAS Olympics!

Remember, BODMAS helps you solve equations in the correct order. Today, we'll practice some basic problems for each part of BODMAS:

Warm-Up Round: Brackets Bonanza!

1. **Tricky Triples:** Solve what's inside the brackets first! $(3 \times 2) + 5 = ?$
2. **Jumping Jacks:** $(7 + 4) \times 3 = ?$

Multiplication Marathon:

1. **Box of Pencils:** You have 4 boxes with 5 pencils each. How many pencils do you have in total? $(4 \times 5) = ?$
2. **Super Sprinting:** Michael runs 3 laps at the track, each lap 100 meters long. What is the total distance he runs? $(3 \times 100) = ?$

Division Dash:

1. **Sharing Cookies:** You have 12 cookies and want to share

them equally with 3 friends. How many cookies does each friend get? $(12 \div 3) = ?$

2. **Balancing Beam:** The balance beam is 6 meters long. If Maya jumps 2 meters at a time, how many jumps does it take her to cross the beam? $(6 \div 2) = ?$

Addition & Subtraction Relay:

1. **Apple Picking:** You pick 7 apples from one tree and 5 apples from another tree. How many apples do you have in total? $(7 + 5) = ?$
2. **Kite Flying Fun:** There are 4 red kites and 3 blue kites flying in the sky. How many kites are there in total? $(4 + 3) = ?$
3. **Pizza Party!** You eat 2 slices of pizza, and your friend eats 1 slice. How many slices are left if there were 8 slices total? $(8 - 2 - 1) = ?$

Bonus Round: BODMAS Challenge!

1. **Hurdle Race:** $(2 \times 3) + (5 \div 1) = ?$ Remember to solve the multiplication first, then the division!

Chapter 16: Shopping Spree with BODMAS!

The BODMAS Bunch's spaceship, the Equationator, was due for a long-overdue maintenance check. But there was a problem - their repair fund was running low. Captain Bracket scratched his head. "We need to buy essential supplies for the repairs, but we have to be smart about it," he declared.

Miss Addition, ever the optimist, chimed in. "Don't worry, Captain! We can use BODMAS to stretch our repair fund as far as possible!"

Intrigued, Sergeant Times, hefted an imaginary shopping bag. "BODMAS for shopping?

How does that work?"

With a mischievous grin, Miss Addition explained their plan. They would create a shopping list of essential repair supplies, but with a twist!

Each item's price would be represented by a BODMAS equation. By solving the equations strategically, they could maximize their purchases within their limited budget.

For example, one item on the list was "Energy Cells" with a price tag of "(2 x 3) + 5." Following BODMAS, they would solve the equation first: 2 x 3 = 6, then add 5, resulting in a final price of 11 credits for the Energy Cells.

They continued down the list, their minds buzzing with calculations. They used multiplication to group similar items (like a pack of 5 bolts), division to get the best deals on bulkier items (like a large can of spaceship grease), and strategic addition and subtraction to ensure they stayed within their budget.

Here's a glimpse of their shopping list:

- **Energy Cells (2 x 3) + 5 credits**
- **Wrench Set (8 / 2) + 3 credits**
- **Box of Bolts (5 x 2) credits**
- **Spaceship Grease (10 - 4) credits**
- **Spare Circuit Board 7 credits**

By the end of their shopping spree, the BODMAS Bunch had managed to procure all the necessary repair supplies and even had a few credits left over for a celebratory space smoothie!

Back at the hangar, Captain Bracket surveyed their loot with a satisfied smile. "Thanks to your brilliant BODMAS plan, Miss Addition, we have everything we need to fix the Equationator and get back on track!"

Miss Addition beamed. "It just goes to show, Captain, that a little math magic can come in handy even on a shopping trip!"

Activity: The BODMAS Bargain Bin!

Calling all young space cadets!

Get ready for a shopping spree at the intergalactic BODMAS Bargain Bin!

What you'll need:

- Worksheet decorated as a space market shopping list.
- The list will include various spaceship repair supplies (energy coils, wires, spaceship lubricant, etc.) with their prices listed as BODMAS equations.
- Play money (or pretend credits)

How to play:

1. Imagine you have a set amount of credits (play money) to spend on spaceship repairs.
2. Browse the shopping list and decide which repair supplies you need.
3. To determine the actual price of each item, you need to solve the BODMAS equation next to it.
4. Keep track of your spending (subtracting the price of each item from your total credits) to ensure you stay within your budget.
5. Once you've solved all the equations, figured out the prices, and stayed within your budget, you've successfully completed your shopping spree at the BODMAS Bargain Bin!

Bonus Challenge: Can you create your own list of repair supplies with BODMAS priced items?

You can even design your shopping list like a space market stall, with fun illustrations and descriptions of the repair supplies!

Let Us Learn the Lesson

Shopping Spree with BODMAS

Get ready for a fantastic shopping adventure!

But wait, there might be some price calculations and discounts to juggle along the way. No worries, because BODMAS (or PEMDAS) is your secret weapon to navigate your shopping spree like a champion!

Shopping Spree Scenarios with BODMAS:

Imagine you're on a shopping spree and encounter these situations:

- **Buy One, Get One Free (BOGO) with a Discount:**
  - A T-shirt costs $10. You buy two and get one free (BOGO). There's also a 10% discount on your entire purchase.

Following BODMAS:

- **Step 1 (Grouping):** Since the BOGO offer applies to buying two T-shirts together, we can consider it a group. Let's say you pay for two initially (2 x $10 = $20).
- **Step 2 (Multiplication):** Apply the discount after finding the initial cost of two T-shirts. 10% discount translates to (10/100) x $20 = $2 (discount amount).
- **Step 3 (Subtraction):** Subtract the discount from the initial cost to find the final price. $20 (initial cost) - $2 (discount) = $18 (total price for two T-shirts).

- **Multiple Items with Different Prices:**
  - You buy a book for $15, a pen for $2, and a notebook for $3.

Following BODMAS:

- **Step 3 (Addition):** Simply add the prices of all the items to find the total cost. $15 (book) + $2 (pen) + $3 (notebook) = $20 (total cost).

- **Calculating Unit Price with Discounts:**

- ◦ A box of cereal is originally priced at $5. There's a promotion where you get $1 off if you buy two boxes.

Following BODMAS:

- **Step 2 (Multiplication):** Since the discount applies when you buy two boxes, calculate the total discount first. $1 (discount per box) x 2 (boxes) = $2 (total discount).
- **Step 3 (Subtraction):** Subtract the total discount from the original price to find the price per box. $5 (original price) - $2 (discount) = $3 (price per box).

Remember:

- BODMAS ensures you perform calculations in the correct order for accurate shopping totals.
- It helps you take advantage of discounts and promotions effectively.
- By understanding BODMAS, you can become a confident and savvy shopper!

Practice Problems:

1. A video game costs $40. There's a 15% discount. How much do you save? (Tip: Use multiplication to find the discount amount.)
2. You buy 3 candy bars at $1 each and a bag of chips for $2. What's the total cost? (Tip: Use addition to find the total cost.)
3. A jacket is priced at $60. You have a $5 coupon. What's the final price you pay? (Tip: Use subtraction to find the final price.)

Congratulations! With BODMAS by your side, you're ready to conquer your shopping sprees and become a math whiz!

Check Your Basic Knowledge

Let's Practice BODMAS on Your Shopping List:

1. **Buy 2, Get 1 Free (BOGO) Bonanza!** A comic book costs $3. You buy 2 and get 1 free (BOGO). How much do you pay in total? (Remember, BOGO is like a group purchase!)
2. **Sticker Savings!** A pack of stickers costs $1. You have a coupon for $0.50 off. How much do you pay after the discount? (Subtraction helps find the final price)
3. **Candy Challenge!** Lollipops are $0.25 each. You buy 4. Gummy bears are $1 each, and you buy 2. How much do you spend on candy in total? (Addition helps find the total cost)
4. **T-Shirt Twister!** A plain T-shirt costs $5. A printed T-shirt costs $7. You buy 2 plain T-shirts and 1 printed T-shirt. What's the total cost? (Remember to add the cost of each type of T-shirt)
5. **Pencil Pouch Party!** A basic pencil pouch costs $2. A fancy pouch with glitter costs $4. You decide on the basic one. How much less expensive is the basic pouch compared to the fancy one? (Subtraction helps find the price difference)
6. **Marble Mania!** A bag of red marbles costs $3. A bag of blue marbles costs $2. You buy both. How much do you spend in total? (Addition helps find the total cost)
7. **Friendship Bracelet Fun!** Craft supplies cost $4. You have $3 saved up already. How much more money do you need to buy the supplies? (Subtraction helps find the remaining amount needed) 8. **Sharing Soda Surprise!** A large soda costs $2. You and your friend decide to share it. How much does each person pay? (Division helps find the cost per person)

8. **Sock Sale!** Socks are originally $4 per pair, but they are on sale for 2 pairs for $6. How much do you save by buying 2 pairs instead of 1? (Use subtraction to find the savings)
9. **Snack Time!** A bag of chips costs $1.50, and a juice box costs $0.75. You buy both for a quick snack. What's the total cost? (Addition helps find the total cost)

Remember: BODMAS helps you solve shopping problems accurately and make the best deals! So have fun shopping and mastering your math skills!

Chapter 17: Cooking with BODMAS!

The BODMAS Bunch was craving a delicious treat after a long day of tinkering with the Equationator. Miss Addition, ever the resourceful chef, decided to whip up a batch of her famous "Cosmic Cookies." But there was a catch - her recipe book was written in a strange code!

"Don't worry, crew," she reassured them. "This looks like a job for BODMAS!"

The recipe for the "Cosmic Cookies" looked like this:

Ingredients:

- **Cosmic Crisps:** (3 x 2) + 1
- **Starry Swirl Sugar:** (8 / 4) - 2
- **Moonbeam Milk:** 5 + (2 x 3)
- **Chocolate Chips:** 10 - (4 / 2)

Sergeant Times, his muscles twitching with anticipation, scratched his head. "Cooking with math?

This is a new one!"

Officer Of, his colon flashing with concentration, piped up. "Remember, crew! BODMAS helps us follow the correct order when measuring ingredients."

With Miss Addition leading the way, they tackled the recipe one ingredient at a time. For the Cosmic Crisps, they first multiplied 3 x 2, resulting in 6. Then, they added 1, giving them a total of 7 Cosmic Crisps for the cookie dough.

They followed the same process for each ingredient, solving the BODMAS equations to determine the precise quantities needed. For the Starry Swirl Sugar, they divided 8 by 4 first, resulting in 2. Then, they subtracted 2, leaving them with a final amount of 0 cups of Starry Swirl Sugar (turns out, the recipe didn't call for any!).

The Moonbeam Milk required a bit more calculation. They added 2 x 3 first, resulting in 6. Then, they added 5, giving them a final amount of 11 cups of Moonbeam Milk.

Finally, for the Chocolate Chips, they divided 4 by 2 first, resulting in 2. Then, they subtracted 2 from 10, leaving them with a perfect amount of 8 delicious Chocolate Chips.

Following the recipe carefully, they mixed, baked, and decorated their Cosmic Cookies. As they enjoyed their warm, gooey treats, the BODMAS Bunch marveled at how math could even be used in the kitchen.

"These cookies are out of this world!" declared Sergeant Times, his mouth full.

Miss Addition beamed. "It just goes to show, BODMAS can be a valuable tool in any situation, even when baking delicious treats!"

Activity: Bake a Batch of BODMAS Biscuits!

Calling all junior space chefs!

Get ready to bake a batch of yummy BODMAS Biscuits with the BODMAS Bunch!

What you'll need:

- Safe and child-friendly recipe for biscuits (cookies) - **Adult supervision is required for any cooking activity!**
- A worksheet with the chosen recipe ingredients listed, but with their quantities represented by BODMAS equations.
- Mixing bowls, spoons, measuring cups, and other baking tools (with adult supervision)

How to play:

1. Work with an adult to ensure safety in the kitchen.
2. Follow the chosen biscuit recipe, but before adding any ingredients, solve the BODMAS equations listed next to each ingredient on the worksheet.
3. The answer to each equation will tell you the exact amount of that ingredient needed for the recipe.
4. With adult supervision, measure and mix the ingredients according to the solved BODMAS equations.
5. Bake your BODMAS Biscuits and enjoy a delicious treat that combines math magic with yummy flavors!

Bonus Challenge: Can you create your own recipe for space-themed treats?

Write the recipe instructions and include BODMAS equations to determine the quantities of each ingredient!

Challenge your friends and family to bake your creation and solve the BODMAS equations to follow the recipe.

Let Us Learn the Lesson

Cooking with BODMAS: Mastering Recipes with Math Magic!

Get ready to become a whiz in the kitchen!

But before you whip up delicious dishes, there might be some measurements and calculations to tackle.

No worries, BODMAS (or PEMDAS in some countries) is your secret ingredient to conquer any recipe with confidence!

Cooking with BODMAS Examples:

- **Double Chocolate Chip Cookies:** The recipe calls for 1 cup of flour and 1/2 cup of chocolate chips. You want to double the recipe. How much flour and chocolate chips do you need?

Following BODMAS:

- **Step 2 (Multiplication):** Double the original amount of each ingredient. Flour: 1 cup x 2 = 2 cups. Chocolate chips: 1/2 cup x 2 = 1 cup.
- You'll need 2 cups of flour and 1 cup of chocolate chips for the doubled recipe.

- **Spicy Stir-Fry Surprise:** The recipe requires 2 chopped onions and 3 chopped bell peppers. You only have 1 onion left. How much additional onion do you need?

Following BODMAS:

- **Step 3 (Subtraction):** Find the difference between the recipe amount and what you have. Needed onions: 2 onions - 1 onion = 1 onion.
- You need to chop 1 additional onion.

- **Mixing Up Milkshakes:** The recipe calls for 1 cup of milk, 1 scoop of ice cream, and 1/2 cup of fruit. You want to make milkshakes for two. How much milk, ice cream, and fruit do you need?

Following BODMAS:

- **Step 2 (Multiplication):** Since you're making for two, multiply each ingredient by 2. Milk: 1 cup x 2 = 2 cups. Ice cream: 1 scoop x 2 = 2 scoops. Fruit: 1/2 cup x 2 = 1 cup.
- You'll need 2 cups of milk, 2 scoops of ice cream, and 1 cup of fruit.

Remember: BODMAS helps you follow recipes precisely, adjust portion sizes, and avoid any kitchen mishaps!

Practice Problems:

1. A recipe calls for 3 eggs. You only have 2. How many more eggs do you need to buy?
2. You want to make half a batch of cookies. The recipe calls for 1 cup of sugar. How much sugar do you need?
3. A cake recipe needs 2 cups of flour and 1/4 cup of baking powder. You're making a smaller cake and only need 3/4 of the recipe. How much flour and baking powder do you need?

Become a Master Chef with BODMAS!

Now you have the tools to conquer any recipe and impress everyone with your culinary skills, all thanks to the magic of BODMAS!

Check Your Basic Knowledge

Let's Practice BODMAS in the Kitchen!

1. **Pancake Party!** The recipe calls for 1 cup of flour and 1/2 cup of milk. You want to make pancakes for two friends, so you need to double the recipe. How much flour and milk do

you need in total? (Multiplication helps find the total amount for two)

2. **Cookie Chaos!** The recipe needs 2 cups of chocolate chips. You only have 1 1/2 cups. How many more cups of chocolate chips do you need to buy? (Subtraction helps find the remaining amount needed)

3. **Sandwich Surprise!** You need 2 slices of bread for a sandwich. You're making sandwiches for yourself and your friend. How many slices of bread do you need in total? (Multiplication helps find the total number of slices)

4. **Pizza Perfection!** The recipe says to use 1/4 cup of tomato sauce for a small pizza. You want to make a medium pizza that needs twice the amount of sauce. How much sauce do you need? (Multiplication helps find the amount for a medium pizza)

5. **Juicy Fun!** A fruit smoothie recipe requires 1 cup of juice and 1/2 cup of fruit. You have 2 cups of juice. How much more fruit do you need if you want to use all the juice? (Subtraction helps find the remaining fruit needed)

6. **Scrumptious Scramble!** You need 2 eggs for scrambled eggs. The recipe also calls for 1/4 cup of chopped vegetables. If you're making scrambled eggs for two people, how many total eggs and cups of vegetables do you need? (Multiplication helps find the total amount for two)

7. **Muffin Mania!** The recipe yields 6 muffins. You only want to make half a batch. The recipe calls for 1 cup of flour for a full batch. How much flour do you need for half a batch? (Division helps find the amount for half the recipe)

8. **Cupcake Confusion!** The recipe needs 3 cups of sugar for a batch of cupcakes. You only have 1 1/2 cups of sugar. What is the difference in sugar needed to complete the recipe? (Subtraction helps find the difference)

9. **Spicy Soup Surprise!** The recipe calls for 1 chopped onion and 2 chopped bell peppers. You only have 1/2 an onion left. How much more onion do you need to chop? (Subtraction helps find the remaining amount needed)

10. **Double Chocolate Chip Delight!** The recipe needs 1 cup of flour and 1/2 cup of chocolate chips. You want to make cookies for your whole family, so you need to triple the recipe. How much flour and chocolate chips do you need in total? (Multiplication helps find the total amount for three times the recipe)

Remember: BODMAS is your secret ingredient for cooking success! So grab your mixing bowls, have fun, and enjoy delicious dishes with the help of BODMAS!

Chapter 18: Building a Branching Out Adventure

A BODMAS Treehouse!

The BODMAS Bunch was itching for a new project. Miss Addition, ever the dreamer, suggested building a magnificent treehouse - a place for stargazing, reading space adventures, and of course, solving BODMAS problems!

Sergeant Times, his muscles rippling with excitement, thumped his fist on the table. "A treehouse! Now that's an idea I can get behind!"

Captain Bracket, the ever-organized leader, knew they needed a plan. "Building a treehouse requires precise measurements, and that's where BODMAS comes in!"

With Miss Addition leading the design, they sketched out their dream treehouse. But instead of using standard measurements, they incorporated BODMAS equations into the design!

Here's a glimpse of their treehouse blueprint:

- **Platform Length:** (4 x 2) + 3 meters
- **Platform Width:** 8 - (2 / 2) meters
- **Ladder Rungs:** (5 + 3) x 2
- **Rope Bridge Length:** (10 x 2) - 4 meters
- **Stargazing Window Diameter:** 5 + (3 / 3) meters

Officer Of, his colon flashing with concentration, surveyed the plans. "This is brilliant!

BODMAS ensures all the parts of the treehouse are built to the correct size."

The BODMAS Bunch got to work, carefully measuring and cutting lumber, rope, and other materials. They used multiplication to calculate the total number of ladder rungs, division to determine the correct rope length for the bridge, and strategic addition and subtraction to ensure all the parts fit together perfectly.

Following their BODMAS blueprint, they constructed a magnificent treehouse. It had a spacious platform, a sturdy ladder, a swinging rope bridge, and a large stargazing window that offered breathtaking views of the night sky.

As they sat in their completed treehouse, gazing at the stars, Miss Addition beamed. "This treehouse is a testament to the power of BODMAS! It's not just about equations – it's about planning, teamwork, and creating something truly special."

Sergeant Times chuckled. "And who knew math could be so much fun?"

Activity: Design Your Dream Treehouse!

Calling all junior architects!

Get ready to design your own spectacular treehouse with the BODMAS Bunch!

What you'll need:

- Large sheet of paper
- Markers, crayons, or colored pencils

- Ruler (optional)

How to play:

- Imagine you're building your dream treehouse! On your paper, sketch out the basic design of your treehouse (platform, ladder, windows, etc.)
- Next to each part of your treehouse design, write a BODMAS equation to determine its measurement.
- Be creative! You can use addition, subtraction, multiplication, and division to come up with interesting measurements for your treehouse features.
- For example, for the platform length, you could write "(3 x 2) + 1 meters" or "8 - (2 / 2) meters".
- Once you've finished your design and BODMAS equations, use your creativity to decorate your treehouse drawing! Add details like furniture, a swing, or a flag!

Bonus Challenge: Can you share your BODMAS treehouse design with a friend or family member?

Challenge them to solve the BODMAS equations to figure out the measurements of your treehouse!

Let Us Learn the Lesson

Building a Branching Out Adventure: A BODMAS Treehouse!

Get ready for a thrilling adventure as you become the architect and builder of your very own treehouse!

But wait, there might be some measurements, angles, and resource allocation to consider.

Don't worry, BODMAS (or PEMDAS in some countries) is your trusty toolbox to navigate the construction process like a pro!

Building with BODMAS:

Imagine you're constructing your awesome treehouse:

- **Planning the Platform**: You need 4 planks of wood, each 3 meters long, for the base. How long will the entire platform be?

Following BODMAS:

- **Step 2 (Multiplication)**: Multiply the length of one plank by the number of planks to find the total platform length. 4 planks x 3 meters/plank = 12 meters.

- **Rope Bridge Challenge**: You need 10 meters of rope to reach the perfect tree branch for the bridge. You already have 5 meters. How much more rope do you need?

Following BODMAS:

- **Step 3 (Subtraction)**: Find the difference between the total rope needed and the amount you already have. 10 meters (needed) - 5 meters (have) = 5 meters (more rope needed).

- **Sharing Supplies:** You have 12 nails and need to share them equally between hammering the platform boards (4 nails) and securing the railings (remaining nails). How many nails will be used for the railings?

Following BODMAS:

- **Step 1 (Grouping):** We can group the nails used for the platform as one task.
- **Step 3 (Subtraction):** Subtract the nails used for the platform from the total to find the remaining nails for the railings. 12 nails (total) - 4 nails (platform) = 8 nails (railings).

Remember: BODMAS helps you tackle construction challenges, manage resources efficiently, and build a fantastic treehouse!

Practice Problems:

1. You buy 3 boards of wood, each 2 meters long, for the treehouse walls. How long is all the wood in total? (Multiplication)
2. The ladder needs 6 rungs spaced 30 centimeters apart. How much total space will the rungs take up? (Multiplication)
3. You have 10 meters of rope. You use 2 meters to secure the swing. How much rope is leftover for other uses? (Subtraction)

With BODMAS by your side, you're ready to build a spectacular treehouse and become a master architect!

So grab your tools, unleash your creativity, and have a blast!

Check Your Basic Knowledge

Let's Practice BODMAS in Your Treehouse Project!

1. **Plank Power!** You need 3 planks of wood, each 2 meters long, for the treehouse floor. How long will the entire floor be? (Use multiplication to find the total length)
2. **Rope Bridge Race!** The perfect tree branch for the bridge is 8 meters away. You have rope that comes in 2-meter sections. How many sections of rope do you need to reach the branch? (Use division to find the number of rope sections)
3. **Nail Navigation!** You have 16 nails for the project. You need 4 nails for the ladder and 3 nails for the trapdoor. How many nails do you have left for other building tasks? (Use subtraction to find the remaining nails)
4. **Window Wonderland!** Each window needs 2 hinges. You plan to have 3 windows. How many hinges do you need in total? (Use multiplication to find the total number of hinges)

5. **Light It Up!** You have a string of lights that is 5 meters long. If you want to add another 2-meter string to reach all the way around the treehouse, how long will the total string be? (Use addition to find the total length)

6. **Compost Creation!** The compost bin needs wooden boards that are each 1 meter long. You need 4 boards for the sides and a top that is 0.5 meters long. How much total wood do you need? (Use addition to find the total length of wood)

7. **Super Shelves!** You plan to build shelves that are each 1.5 meters long. If you want to have 2 shelves stacked on top of each other, what will be the total length of the shelves? (Use multiplication to find the total length)

8. **Leftover Lumber!** You buy 6 boards of wood, each 2 meters long, for the walls. After construction, you have 1 meter of leftover wood. What was the total length of the wood before you had any leftovers? (Use subtraction to find the original total length)

9. **Sharing Seeds!** You have 10 packets of flower seeds and want to share them equally with 2 friends. How many packets will each person get? (Use division to find the number of packets per person)

10. **Stargazing Surprise!** The roof window is 1 meter wide. You want to add curtains that are 1.5 meters wide on each side. How wide will the total window covering be? (Use multiplication to find the total width of the curtains, then add that to the window width)

Remember: BODMAS is your secret weapon for building a fantastic treehouse! So have fun constructing, and enjoy your awesome creation!

Chapter 19: A BODMAS Bash!

The BODMAS Bunch was buzzing with excitement. It was Captain Bracket's birthday, and they were planning a surprise party - a celebration filled with laughter, games, and of course, delicious food!

Miss Addition, ever the meticulous planner, decided to utilize BODMAS to ensure a successful party within their budget. "Let's make this a BODMAS Bash!" she declared.

Sergeant Times, his muscles twitching with enthusiasm, scratched his head. "BODMAS for parties? How does that work?"

With a mischievous grin, Miss Addition explained their plan. They would create a party plan with various elements, but with a twist!

Each element, from decorations to food quantities, would have a cost represented by a BODMAS equation. By solving the equations strategically, they could maximize their fun within their budget.

For example, one item on their list was "Starry Streamers" with a cost of "(2 x 3) + 4 credits." Following BODMAS, they would solve the equation first: 2 x 3 = 6, then add 4, resulting in a final cost of 10 credits for the Starry Streamers.

They continued down the list, calculating decoration costs, party game supplies, and most importantly, food quantities!

They used multiplication to determine the total amount of space-themed snacks needed for the entire crew (based on the number of guests), division to figure out the right amount of ingredients for a giant pot of space punch, and strategic addition and subtraction to ensure they stayed within their budget.

Here's a glimpse of their party plan:

- **Starry Streamers: (2 x 3) + 4 credits**
- **Cosmic Confetti: (8 / 2) - 2 credits**
- **Space Punch (serves 5): (3 x 2) + 1 litres**
- **Meteor Munchies (serves 5): (5 x 4) / 2 bags**
- **Intergalactic Games: 10 credits**

By the end of their planning session, the BODMAS Bunch had a fantastic party plan, all within their budget!

They decorated the spaceship with shimmering streamers and cosmic confetti, prepared a giant pot of space punch, and gathered enough Meteor Munchies for the whole crew.

The party was a huge success, filled with laughter, games, and delicious treats. Captain Bracket, overwhelmed by the surprise and the incredible party, beamed with joy.

"This is the best birthday ever!" he declared. "Thanks to your brilliant BODMAS planning, Miss Addition, we had a fantastic celebration!"

Miss Addition winked. "It just goes to show, Captain, a little math magic can make any party truly out of this world!"

Activity: Plan Your Super Stellar Soiree!

Calling all junior party planners!

Get ready to throw a super stellar soiree with the BODMAS Bunch!

What you'll need:

- Worksheet decorated as a party planning checklist.
- The list will include various party elements (decorations, food, games) with their costs listed as BODMAS equations.
- Play money (or pretend credits)

How to play:

1. Imagine you have a set amount of credits (play money) to spend on your party.
2. Browse the party planning checklist and decide what decorations, food, and games you want for your party.
3. To determine the actual cost of each item, you need to solve the BODMAS equation next to it.
4. Keep track of your spending (subtracting the price of each item from your total credits) to ensure you stay within your budget.
5. Once you've solved all the equations, figured out the prices, and stayed within your budget, you've successfully planned your super stellar soiree!

Bonus Challenge: Can you create your own list of party elements with BODMAS priced items?

You can even design your checklist like a party invitation, with fun illustrations and descriptions of the decorations, food, and games!

Let Us Learn the Lesson

BODMAS Bash: A Fun and Competitive Way to Master Order of Operations!

Get ready for a thrilling BODMAS Bash, a competition where you become a math whiz and BODMAS (PEMDAS in some countries) is your ultimate weapon!

BODMAS Bash is like a math Olympics where you compete in challenges that test your skills in using BODMAS correctly. It's a fun and engaging way to learn and practice this important concept.

Here's how BODMAS Bash might work:

1. **Warm-Up Round: Bracket Blitz!**
   - Teams race to solve problems that involve calculations within brackets. They need to solve what's inside the brackets first before proceeding with the rest of the equation.

2. **Multiplication Marathon:**
   - Teams compete to solve equations with the most multiplications in the shortest time. Speed and accuracy are key!

3. **Division Dash:**
   - This event focuses on division problems. Teams race to find the correct answers, demonstrating their understanding of division within BODMAS.

4. **Addition & Subtraction Relay:**
   - Teams take turns solving problems involving addition and subtraction, passing the baton (or answer) to the next teammate. The first team to finish the relay race with all answers correct wins.

5. **The BODMAS Battle Royale:**
   - The ultimate test! This final round combines all aspects of BODMAS. Teams tackle complex equations that involve multiple operations. They need to follow the correct order of operations to emerge victorious.

Benefits of BODMAS Bash:

- **Makes learning BODMAS fun and interactive.**
- **Provides a competitive yet enjoyable way to practice math skills.**
- **Encourages teamwork, communication, and problem-solving abilities.**
- **Boosts confidence and celebrates the joy of math.**

So, grab your calculators (optional!), put on your thinking caps, and get ready to participate in the exciting world of BODMAS Bash!

Now for an Extra Twist: Points and Rewards!

- Each round can award points based on speed, accuracy, and teamwork.
- The winning team at the end of the BODMAS Bash gets bragging rights and a special reward (maybe candy or a small prize!).

Remember: BODMAS Bash is all about celebrating math and learning in a fun and competitive way. So, have fun, challenge yourself, and become a BODMAS champion!

Check Your Basic Knowledge

BODMAS Bash Practice Problems: Sharpen Your Math Skills!

Welcome to the exciting BODMAS Bash! Remember, BODMAS helps you solve equations in the correct order.

Today, we'll tackle some basic problems for each part of BODMAS to prepare you for the challenges:

Warm-Up Round: Bracket Blitz!

1. **Tricky Triples:** Solve what's inside the brackets first! $(2 \times 3) + 5 = ?$
2. **Jumping Jacks:** $(4 + 7) \times 2 = ?$

Multiplication Marathon:

1. **Box of Crayons:** You have 3 boxes with 6 crayons each. How many crayons do you have in total? (3 x 6) = ?
2. **Super Sprinting:** Michael runs 2 laps at the track, each lap 100 meters long. What is the total distance he runs? (2 x 100) = ?

Division Dash:

1. **Sharing Cookies:** You have 12 cookies and want to share them equally with 2 friends. How many cookies does each friend get? (12 ÷ 2) = ?
2. **Balancing Beam:** The balance beam is 4 meters long. If Maya jumps 2 meters at a time, how many jumps does it take her to cross the beam? (4 ÷ 2) = ?

Addition & Subtraction Relay:

1. **Apple Picking:** You pick 5 apples from one tree and 3 apples from another tree. How many apples do you have in total? (5 + 3) = ?
2. **Kite Flying Fun:** There are 2 red kites and 4 blue kites flying in the sky. How many kites are there in total? (2 + 4) = ?
3. **Pizza Party!** You eat 2 slices of pizza, and your friend eats 1 slice. How many slices are left if there were 8 slices total? (8 - 2 - 1) = ?

Bonus Round: BODMAS Challenge!

1. **Hurdle Race:** (3 x 2) + (6 ÷ 2) = ? Remember to solve the multiplication first, then the division!

Chapter 20: BODMAS Saves the Day!

The bustling marketplace of Mega City 1000 was in chaos. A malfunctioning delivery drone zipped erratically through the crowds, its cargo bay door hanging open and spewing out packages like confetti. People scattered in all directions, narrowly avoiding falling boxes and whirring propellers.

Suddenly, a figure streaked through the marketplace, a red cape billowing behind them. It was Bodmas, the defender of mathematical meltdowns!

Their bright yellow costume, emblazoned with a plus sign, minus sign, multiplication symbol, and division symbol, announced their identity.

Bodmas landed gracefully in front of the malfunctioning drone. Its metallic voice shrieked, "Power Cell Failure! Emergency Landing Procedures Initiated!"

"Don't worry, little drone," boomed Bodmas' voice, a reassuring echo of their amplified helmet. "I'll get you under control."

With a practiced eye, Bodmas scanned the drone's control panel. It was a mess of flashing lights and nonsensical error codes. But then, Bodmas spotted it - a blinking sequence of numbers and symbols:

"7 + (3 x 2) = Error"

Bodmas's brow furrowed. This was a BODMAS emergency! The drone's control system was malfunctioning because it couldn't solve a simple equation.

Taking a deep breath, Bodmas shouted out the answer, "The answer is 13! That's the correct control code!"

As if by magic, the error code vanished from the panel. The drone's whirring calmed, and its cargo bay door shut with a reassuring thud.

Relief washed over the marketplace crowd. People cheered for Bodmas, the hero who saved them from a package avalanche. The grateful delivery drone beeped its thanks and zipped away, its deliveries back on track.

Later, at Bodmas's secret headquarters (a cozy attic apartment above a math bookstore), Bodmas reflected on the day's events.

"It just goes to show," Bodmas thought, a smile spreading under their mask, "BODMAS isn't just about numbers and equations. It's about using your mind to solve problems, big or small. And sometimes, all it takes is a little superhero math magic to save the day!"

Activity: Design Your BODMAS Superhero!

Calling all junior crime fighters!

It's your turn to create your own BODMAS superhero!

What you'll need:

- Large sheet of paper
- Markers, crayons, or colored pencils
- Scissors (optional)
- Construction paper (optional)

- Tape or glue (optional)

How to play:

1. Imagine your own BODMAS superhero! What kind of costume would they wear? What would their special powers be (related to BODMAS, of course!)
2. On your paper, draw your BODMAS superhero. You can give them a cool costume that incorporates BODMAS symbols (plus sign, minus sign, multiplication symbol, division symbol). They can also have a utility belt with pouches or compartments labeled with BODMAS symbols.
3. Get creative! Think about what kind of problems your BODMAS superhero would solve. Maybe they can use multiplication to build giant bridges or division to distribute food supplies equally in a crisis.
4. (Optional) If you want to make a BODMAS superhero mask or costume accessory, you can use construction paper, tape, and scissors to bring your design to life!

Bonus Challenge: Can you write a short story about your BODMAS superhero?

Describe a situation where they use their BODMAS powers to save the day!

Remember, the problem they solve can be anything, but the solution should involve using BODMAS in a creative way.

Let Us Learn the Lesson

BODMAS Saves the Day: A Superhero for Solving Math Problems!

Imagine yourself as a superhero, but instead of fighting villains, you battle incorrect math solutions!

Your secret weapon?

BODMAS is like your superhero suit, ensuring you solve math problems in the correct order and achieve perfect results. Here's how it saves the day in different situations:

1. Baking Bonanza:

You're baking cookies for a party, and the recipe calls for 2 cups of flour and 1/2 cup of chocolate chips. You want to double the recipe, but if you don't follow BODMAS, disaster strikes!

(Incorrect way: 2 cups + 1/2 cup) x 2 = 5 cups (wrong total!)

Following BODMAS: (2 cups x 2) + (1/2 cup x 2) = 4 cups + 1 cup = 5 cups (correct total!)

2. Shopping Spree Surprise:

You're at a store that has a sale on T-shirts: buy 2, get 1 free! You pick out 2 shirts at $5 each. Without BODMAS, you might overpay!

(Incorrect way: 2 x $5) + ($5 free) = $10 (too much!)

Following BODMAS: 2 x $5 = $10 (initial cost) - $0 (free shirt) = $10 (correct price)

3. Treasure Hunt Time:

A treasure map tells you to walk 3 steps forward, then turn left and walk (2 x 4) steps. If you don't use BODMAS, you might end up in the wrong spot!

(Incorrect way: 3 + 2) x 4 = 20 steps (wrong direction!)

Following BODMAS: 2 x 4 = 8 steps (turn left first) + 3 steps = 11 steps (correct direction)

Remember: BODMAS ensures you are a confident and accurate math superhero! It helps you avoid mistakes and achieve success in all sorts of situations.

Become a BODMAS Master!

By understanding BODMAS, you can conquer any math problem that comes your way. Practice your skills, and soon, you'll be solving equations like a true superhero!

Check Your Basic Knowledge

Let's see how BODMAS saves the day in different situations:

1. **Pizza Party Panic!** You need to order enough pizza for your friends. The recipe says 1 cup of flour makes 1 pizza. You want to make 2 pizzas, but if you don't use BODMAS, you might not order enough flour! (Use multiplication to find the total flour needed)

2. **Sticker Sharing Showdown!** You have 12 stickers and want to share them equally with 2 friends. If you don't use BODMAS, you might not give everyone a fair share! (Use division to find the number of stickers per person)

3. **Candy Caper!** Lollipops are $0.25 each, and you buy 4. Gummy bears are $1 each, and you buy 2. Without BODMAS, you might not know the total cost! (Use addition to find the total cost)

4. **Movie Marathon Mayhem!** A movie is 2 hours long, and you watch it 3 times. If you don't use BODMAS, you might underestimate how much time you spent watching! (Use multiplication to find the total watch time)

5. **Juice Box Juggle!** You have a 6-pack of juice boxes, but you drink 2 right away. Without BODMAS, you might not know how many are left! (Use subtraction to find the remaining juice boxes)

6. **Sock Sale Savings!** Socks are originally $4 per pair, but they are on sale for 2 pairs for $6. If you don't use BODMAS, you might not know how much you save! (Use subtraction to find the savings)

7. **Friendship Bracelet Frenzy!** Craft supplies cost $4. You have $3 saved up already. Without BODMAS, you might not know how much more money you need! (Use subtraction to find the remaining amount needed)

8. **Sharing Soda Surprise!** A large soda costs $2. You and your friend decide to share it. If you don't use BODMAS, you might not know how much each person pays! (Use division

to find the cost per person)

9. **Building Block Bonanza!** You have 10 blocks, and your friend has 5. If you don't use BODMAS, you might not know the total number of blocks to play with! (Use addition to find the total number of blocks)

10. **Snack Time Scramble!** A bag of chips costs $1.50, and a juice box costs $0.75. You buy both for a quick snack. If you don't use BODMAS, you might not know the total cost! (Use addition to find the total cost)

Remember: BODMAS is your secret weapon for solving math problems! So be a math hero, use BODMAS, and always get the correct answer!

Chapter 21: BODMAS Brain Benders!

The BODMAS Bunch was on a routine mission to deliver supplies to a remote lunar research station. As they approached the station, however, a strange message crackled through their communication system:

"Greetings, travelers. Passage to the station is blocked. To unlock the access code, you must solve the BODMAS Brain Benders!"

A holographic display flickered to life, revealing a series of cryptic puzzles. Captain Bracket, ever the leader, rallied the crew. "Looks like we need to put our BODMAS skills to the test!" he declared.

The first puzzle was a maze of colored squares. Each square held a number or a symbol (+, -, x, /). To navigate the maze and reach the exit, they had to follow a specific path. The path could only turn right if the sum of the two numbers/symbols in the current and next square was even, and left if the sum was odd.

Miss Addition, a whiz at calculations, took charge. She meticulously analyzed the maze, adding the values in adjacent squares to determine the right direction. After a few wrong turns and clever calculations, they navigated the maze and emerged victorious.

The next challenge was a series of locked doors, each labeled with a BODMAS equation and a number. Only the door with the answer matching the displayed number would unlock. Sergeant Times, muscles tensed with concentration, tackled this challenge. He meticulously solved each equation, following BODMAS order, to find the door with the matching answer. With each solved equation and unlocked door, they inched closer to the research station.

The final challenge was a set of cryptic instructions. It involved rearranging a series of scrambled words to form a sentence, with the order determined by BODMAS. Officer Of, his colon flashing with concentration, meticulously analyzed the scrambled words. He noticed that some words contained BODMAS symbols. Following the order of operations (division, multiplication, addition, subtraction), he rearranged the words to form a sentence that revealed the final access code.

With a triumphant cry, they entered the access code, and the doors to the research station slid open. Relief washed over the crew. They had conquered the BODMAS Brain Benders and ensured the safe delivery of their supplies.

"Those puzzles certainly tested our BODMAS mettle!" exclaimed Miss Addition, wiping sweat from her brow.

Captain Bracket smiled. "Indeed! But just goes to show, with teamwork and a good grasp of BODMAS, we can overcome any obstacle."

Activity: The BODMAS Brain Maze!

Calling all junior puzzle masters!

Can you help the BODMAS Bunch navigate the BODMAS Brain Maze and reach the research station?

What you'll need:

- Maze printout with squares containing numbers and BODMAS symbols (+, -, x, /)
- Pencil

How to play:

1. Start at the entrance of the BODMAS Brain Maze.
2. As you move through the maze, you can only turn right if the sum of the two numbers/symbols in the current and next square is even.
3. If the sum is odd, you must turn left.
4. Use your BODMAS skills to add the values in adjacent squares to determine the right direction.
5. Reach the exit of the maze to help the BODMAS Bunch access the research station!

Bonus Challenge: Can you create your own BODMAS Brain Maze?

Design the maze layout and fill the squares with numbers and symbols.

Remember, the path through the maze should only be possible by following the BODMAS rule for turning directions (even sum = right turn, odd sum = left turn).

Let Us Learn the Lesson

BODMAS Brain Benders: Challenge Your Math Muscles!

Get ready to test your BODMAS (PEMDAS in some countries) skills with some mind-bending problems!

BODMAS, like a mental gymnastics routine for math, ensures you solve equations in the correct order for an accurate answer.

BODMAS Brain Benders will push your understanding of order of operations and make you a true math champion!

The Challenge:

These problems might look a little different from usual. They might have missing information, require some creative thinking, or seem a bit tricky at first glance. But don't worry, with your BODMAS knowledge, you can crack the code!

Examples of BODMAS Brain Benders:

1. **Missing Math Mystery:** The answer to this equation is 11. Can you figure out the missing number and operation to make it true: _ + 3 x 2 = 11? (Hint: Use multiplication first, then addition)

2. **Word Problem Whirlwind:** John has 4 apples, but Sarah takes 2 away. He then buys 3 more apples. How many apples does John have now? (This problem involves multiple steps that require using subtraction and then addition)

3. **Tricky Time Travel:** It takes a spaceship 8 hours to travel to a new planet, and the astronauts spend 2 hours exploring. If the return trip also takes 8 hours, what is the total travel time? (Be careful not to add the exploration time to just one travel leg!)

4. **Double the Dilemma:** A recipe yields 6 cookies. If you double the recipe, what is the total number of cookies? (Remember, doubling involves multiplication)

5. **Leftover Logic:** You buy 10 meters of rope, but only need 7 meters for a project. How many meters of rope are leftover? (This is a simple subtraction problem)

Remember: BODMAS Brain Benders are designed to challenge you and make you think critically. Don't be afraid to experiment with different approaches and use your BODMAS knowledge to find the correct solution!

Bonus Tip: Read the problem carefully and identify the key information and operations involved. Then, apply BODMAS step-by-step to reach the answer.

Ready to become a BODMAS Brain Bender master?

Grab your thinking cap and get started!

Check Your Basic Knowledge

Let's Test Your BODMAS Skills!

1. **Pizza Party Puzzle:** You need 1 cup of flour for 1 pizza. You want to make pizzas for 3 friends and yourself. How much flour do you need in total? (Use multiplication to find the total flour needed)

2. **Sharing Stickers Secret:** You have 16 stickers and want to share them equally with 2 friends. If you don't use BODMAS, you might not give everyone a fair share! (Use division to find the number of stickers per person)

3. **Candy Caper Conundrum:** Lollipops are $0.50 each, and you buy 3. Gummy bears are $1 each, and you buy 2. Without BODMAS, you might not know the total cost! (Use multiplication for each type of candy, then add the totals)

4. **Movie Marathon Mystery:** A movie is 2 hours long, but you watch it with a friend and decide to take a 30-minute break in the middle. If you don't use BODMAS, you might underestimate how much time you spent watching! (Use multiplication to find the movie watch time, then add the break time)

5. **Juice Box Juggle Challenge:** You have a 6-pack of juice boxes, but you and your friend drink 2 right away. Without BODMAS, you might not know how many are left! (Use subtraction to find the remaining juice boxes)

6. **Sock Sale Surprise:** Socks are originally $4 per pair, but they

are on sale for buy 2, get 1 free. If you don't use BODMAS, you might not know the actual price per pair! (Think about how many pairs you get for the sale price, then divide the total cost by the number of pairs)

7. **Friendship Bracelet Frenzy:** Craft supplies cost $5. You have $2 saved up already. Without BODMAS, you might not know how much more money you need! (Use subtraction to find the remaining amount needed)

8. **Sharing Soda Spoilsports:** A large soda costs $2. You, your friend, and your sibling decide to share it. If you don't use BODMAS, you might not know how much each person pays! (Use division to find the cost per person)

9. **Building Block Bonanza:** You have 8 blocks, your friend has 3, and your sibling has 2. If you don't use BODMAS, you might not know the total number of blocks to play with! (Use addition to find the total number of blocks)

10. **Snack Time Scramble:** A bag of chips costs $1.25, and a juice box costs $0.75. You buy both for a quick snack. If you don't use BODMAS, you might not know the total cost! (Use addition to find the total cost)

Remember: BODMAS is your key to unlocking the secrets of math problems. So use your detective skills, follow BODMAS, and become a master of brain-bending challenges!

Chapter 22: Multiplication Mash!

In the bustling Robo-Repair Shop of Mega City 1000, a friendly rivalry buzzed between the resident repair bots. Every Friday afternoon, they put down their wrenches and screwdrivers for a high-octane competition - the Multiplication Mash!

Rusty, the veteran bot with a paint job as chipped as his circuits, was known for his methodical approach. He calculated each answer with precision, his gears whirring thoughtfully.

Beeper, the sleek new arrival with flashing lights and a smooth chassis, relied on his lightning-fast processors. He zipped through the multiplication problems at breakneck speed, beeps and whirs forming a continuous stream.

Today's Multiplication Mash was no ordinary competition. The challenge was set by Miss Millie, the kind but firm owner of the Robo-Repair Shop.

"Alright, bots," boomed Miss Millie, her voice echoing through the workshop. "Today's Mash will test not just speed, but also accuracy!

We'll start with simple problems and gradually increase the difficulty."

A holographic screen flickered to life, displaying the first set of multiplication problems:

- $2 \times 3 = ?$
- $5 \times 1 = ?$
- $4 \times 4 = ?$

Rusty took his time, his internal calculator whirring softly. Beeper, on the other hand, buzzed with anticipation.

As soon as the problems appeared, Beeper blurted out the answers in a rapid-fire sequence: "Six! Five! Sixteen!"

Miss Millie smiled. "Impressive speed, Beeper!

But let's see if your answers are correct."

One by one, Miss Millie confirmed Beeper's answers. He was right on all counts!

The difficulty level increased as the Mash progressed. Soon, the problems involved larger numbers and trickier calculations:

- $7 \times 8 = ?$
- $9 \times 12 = ?$
- $6 \times 6 = ?$

Rusty, ever the methodical one, took his sweet time, ensuring his calculations were flawless. Beeper, still buzzing with competitive energy, continued his rapid-fire approach.

The final round was a nail-biter. Both bots faced a series of complex multiplication problems, pushing their processors to the limit.

In the end, it was a tie! Rusty's accuracy and Beeper's speed resulted in a perfect score for both of them.

Miss Millie beamed with pride. "Congratulations, boys! You both showed incredible skill in the Multiplication Mash!"

Rusty and Beeper, despite the competition, exchanged a friendly whirring sound, a sign of mutual respect. They had learned that both speed and accuracy were important when it came to mastering multiplication.

From that day on, the Multiplication Mash became a cherished tradition at the Robo-Repair Shop. It was a reminder that even robots could learn, compete, and most importantly, have fun with math!

Activity: Multiplication Mash Up!

Calling all junior math whizzes!

Get ready for your own Multiplication Mash Up with Rusty and Beeper!

What you'll need:

- Two sets of multiplication flashcards (one for you, one for a friend or family member) - You can create your own flashcards or use store-bought ones.
- Timer (optional)

How to play:

1. Challenge a friend or family member to a friendly Multiplication Mash Up!
2. Shuffle your set of multiplication flashcards.
3. Decide on the number of rounds and the difficulty level of the flashcards (start with easier problems and gradually increase difficulty).
4. Set a timer (optional) for each round.
5. When the timer starts (or when you're both ready), each of you should try to answer the multiplication problems on your flashcards as quickly and accurately as possible.
6. After each round, check each other's answers. The player with

the most correct answers in the least amount of time wins the round!

7. Play multiple rounds to see who emerges as the ultimate Multiplication Mash Up champion!

Bonus Challenge: Can you create your own set of multiplication flashcards with challenging problems?

You can include multiplication problems with larger numbers or even introduce trickier concepts like multiplication by 0 or 1.

Let Us Learn the Lesson

Multiplication Mash: Turning Times Tables into a Bop!

Multiplication can sometimes feel like a boring drill, but what if we could turn it into a fun and energetic experience?

Enter Multiplication Mash!

Multiplication Mash is a dynamic approach to learning multiplication tables that combines music, movement, and a dash of friendly competition.

Think of it as a dance party where you celebrate your multiplication skills!

Here's how Multiplication Mash works:

1. **Pick a Pumped-Up Playlist:** Choose some energetic music with a clear beat. Popular songs, movie soundtracks, or even catchy children's music can all work!

2. **Move and Multiply:** Assign different multiplication facts to specific body movements. For example, jumping 3 times could represent the 3 times tables (3 x 1 = 3, jump once; 3 x 2 = 6, jump twice, and so on).

3. **Get Grooving:** As the music plays, the leader (teacher, parent, or even a student!) calls out multiplication problems. Everyone moves according to the assigned body movements for that specific fact.

4. **Level Up:** Start with easier multiplication tables and

gradually increase the difficulty as everyone gets more comfortable. You can even have group challenges where teams compete to perform the movements correctly.

5. **Make it Fun!** Introduce fun props like colorful scarves or wear silly hats to add a playful element to the learning experience.

Benefits of Multiplication Mash:

- **Engages multiple learning styles:** Combines auditory (hearing the music), kinesthetic (moving the body), and visual (seeing the movements) learning styles.
- **Makes learning multiplication interactive and fun:** Transforms drills into an enjoyable activity.
- **Boosts memory and recall:** Physical movement helps solidify multiplication facts in the mind.
- **Encourages teamwork and participation:** Creates a positive learning environment where everyone can participate.

So, turn up the volume, grab your imaginary microphone (or a real one!), and get ready to mash those multiplication tables into your memory!

Bonus Tip: You can create your own Multiplication Mash routines or find inspiration online for pre-made activities and challenges.

Check Your Basic Knowledge

Multiplication Mash: BODMAS Boogie!

Get ready to move and groove while mastering BODMAS (PEMDAS in some countries) with Multiplication Mash!

This time, we'll combine multiplying with BODMAS to create a funky learning experience.

Multiplication Mash: BODMAS Edition

Here's how it works: We'll have different moves for each part of BODMAS and multiplication facts!

- **Jump:** This represents multiplication (jump once for 1 times tables, twice for 2 times tables, etc.)
- **Spin:** This represents division (spin once for dividing by 2, twice for dividing by 4, etc.)
- **High Five:** This represents addition (high five a friend for each number added)
- **Touch Toes:** This represents subtraction (touch your toes once for subtracting 1, twice for subtracting 2, etc.)

The BODMAS Boogie:

The leader calls out an equation. Everyone performs the moves based on the order of operations (BODMAS) in the equation!

Let's Practice!

1. **Problem:** 2 x 3 + 1 (Move:** Jump twice (2 x 3), High Five once (+1))
2. **Problem:** 4 / 2 + 3 (Move:** Spin twice (4 / 2), High Five three times (+ 3))
3. **Problem:** 1 + 5 x 2 (Move:** High Five once (+ 1), Jump twice (5 x 2))
4. **Problem:** 6 - 2 x 1 (Move:** Touch toes twice (6 - 2), Jump once (x 1))
5. **Problem:** 3 x (2 + 1) (Move imaginary brackets! Jump twice inside the brackets first (2 + 1), then jump three times for the entire equation (3 x 3))

Ready to Mash Up Your Math Skills?

This is just a starting point!

You can create your own BODMAS moves or challenges. Multiplication Mash with BODMAS makes learning fun, energetic, and helps you master your math skills in no time!

Chapter 23: Division Dash!

A thrilling buzz filled the corridors of the Galactic Grand Prix Arena. Today was the annual Division Dash, a race for the bravest cadets in the Intergalactic Academy.

The goal: navigate a challenging obstacle course filled with division problems, all while maintaining the fastest time.

Among the competitors were our favorite heroes, the BODMAS Bunch. Miss Addition, ever the strategist, carefully reviewed the course layout. Sergeant Times, muscles twitching with anticipation, bounced on his metallic feet. Officer Of, his colon flashing with concentration, was already formulating calculations in his mind.

The starting signal echoed through the arena. The cadets bolted forward, a blur of colorful jumpsuits. The first obstacle was a series of laser beams spaced unevenly across the corridor. A holographic display above each beam flashed a division problem:

- 12 / 3 = ? (3 beams)
- 16 / 4 = ? (4 beams)
- 10 / 2 = ? (5 beams)

To deactivate the lasers and proceed, the cadets had to solve the division problem and jump over the corresponding number of beams. Miss Addition, with her lightning-fast mental math, zipped past the lasers with ease. Sergeant Times, relying on brute strength, attempted to jump over all the beams at once, but tripped and activated a few lasers, losing precious seconds.

The next challenge was a climbing wall, but the handholds were missing! Instead, there were panels displaying division problems:

- 20 / 5 = ? (This panel had 5 handholds)
- 18 / 3 = ? (This panel had 6 handholds)
- 24 / 4 = ? (This panel had 6 handholds)

The cadets had to solve the problem and climb the wall using the number of handholds indicated by the answer. Officer Of, his methodical approach proving valuable, meticulously calculated the answers and scaled the wall with impressive speed. Miss Addition, impatient as always, attempted to climb a wall with fewer handholds than the answer, but lost her grip and fell back down.

The final obstacle was a memory maze. The cadets had to navigate a series of branching paths, but only one path led to the finish line. Each branch point displayed a division problem:

- 36 / 9 = ? (Left path)
- 28 / 7 = ? (Right path)

The correct answer led to the next section of the maze, while the wrong answer led to a dead end. Sergeant Times, relying on his gut instinct, took a wrong turn at the first junction and wasted valuable time backtracking. Miss Addition, ever the problem solver, used her memory to recall the answers from previous obstacles and navigated the maze flawlessly.

In the end, it was a close race. But Miss Addition, with her combination of speed and accuracy, emerged victorious! The crowd erupted in cheers as she crossed the finish line, a triumphant smile lighting up her face.

Sergeant Times, catching his breath after a grueling race, approached Miss Addition with a grin. "You were amazing, Addition! Guess brains do win races after all."

Miss Addition chuckled. "It wasn't all about brains, Times. A little teamwork and a healthy dose of BODMAS skills go a long way too!"

From that day on, the Division Dash became a legendary event at the Intergalactic Academy, a reminder that math skills could be the key to success, even in a high-octane race.

Activity: The Division Dash Challenge!

Calling all future space cadets!

Get ready for your own Division Dash Challenge with the BODMAS Bunch!

What you'll need:

- Maze printout with branching paths and division problems at each junction point.
- Pencil

How to play:

1. Imagine you're a cadet participating in the Division Dash! Your goal is to navigate the maze and reach the finish line as quickly as possible.
2. As you reach each junction point in the maze, you'll encounter a division problem.
3. Solve the division problem to determine which path (left or right) leads you closer to the finish line.

4. The correct answer will lead you to the next section of the maze, while the wrong answer will lead you to a dead end, forcing you to backtrack and try again.
5. Use your division skills and problem-solving abilities to navigate the maze and reach the finish line!

Bonus Challenge: Can you create your own Division Dash maze? Design the layout of the maze and include division problems at each junction point. Make sure the answer to each problem determines which path leads to the next section of the maze and avoids dead ends.

Let Us Learn the Lesson

Division Dash: A Race to Sharpen Your Sharing Skills!

Calling all math whizzes!

Get ready for Division Dash, a fast-paced and exciting competition designed to test your division skills.

It's like a race track for division problems, where speed and accuracy are key!

Division is all about sharing things fairly. In Division Dash, you'll put your sharing skills to the test by solving division problems as quickly as possible.

Here's how Division Dash works:

1. **Get Set, Go!** Participants gather in teams or compete individually.
2. **Division Challenges:** The leader displays division problems on a board or screen. These problems can involve whole numbers, decimals, or fractions, depending on the difficulty level.
3. **Race to the Answer:** Everyone uses their math skills to solve the problems as quickly as possible. You can use scrap paper or whiteboards to write down your calculations.
4. **First Past the Finish Line:** The first person (or team) to solve the problem correctly wins the round and earns points.

5. **Variety is the Spice of Dash!** The leader can mix things up by including:
    - **Word problems:** These problems involve real-life scenarios that require division to find the answer.
    - **Relay races:** Teams take turns solving parts of a division problem, passing the "answer baton" to the next teammate.
    - **Bonus challenges:** These could involve solving multiple division problems in a row or finding the missing number in a division equation.

Benefits of Division Dash:

- **Makes learning division fun and engaging:** Transforms drills into a competitive activity.
- **Improves mental math skills:** Encourages quick thinking and problem-solving under pressure.
- **Boosts teamwork and communication (in team settings):** Requires communication and collaboration to solve problems efficiently.
- **Provides a positive learning environment:** Celebrates the joy of math and learning.

So, grab your imaginary racing helmet (or a real one!), sharpen your division skills, and get ready to Division Dash your way to math mastery!

Bonus Tip: You can practice division problems beforehand or use online resources to find a variety of division challenges for different difficulty levels.

Check Your Basic Knowledge

Division Dash: BODMAS Race to the Finish!

Get ready for a thrilling Division Dash competition!

But wait, there might be some tricky calculations with division and other operations.

Let's see how BODMAS helps in Division Dash!

1. **Pizza Party Challenge:** There are 12 slices of pizza, and you want to share them equally with 2 friends. How many slices do you each get? (Use division to find the number of slices per person)

2. **Jump Rope Race:** There are 10 meters of jump rope, and you want to cut it into 2 equal pieces for you and your friend. How long will each piece be? (Use division to find the length of each rope)

3. **Candy Sharing Spree:** You have 16 candies and want to give 4 to each of your 2 friends. How many candies do you have leftover? (Use division first to find the number of candies given away, then subtraction to find the leftover candies)

4. **Juice Box Juggle:** There are 6 juice boxes, and you drink 2 right away. Then you buy 3 more. How many juice boxes do you have in total now? (Use subtraction first to find the remaining juice boxes after drinking, then addition to find the total after buying more)

5. **Sticker Stack Surprise:** You have 5 sheets of stickers with 4 stickers on each sheet. How many stickers do you have in total? (Use multiplication to find the total number of stickers, then you've solved the problem without needing division!)

6. **Sock Sale Savings:** Socks are originally $4 per pair, but they are on sale for 2 pairs for $6. What is the cost per pair on sale? (Use division to find the price per pair)

7. **Friendship Bracelet Bonanza!** Craft supplies cost $7. You already saved $3. Do you have enough money to buy the supplies? (Use subtraction to find the remaining amount needed)

8. **Sharing Soda Sprint:** A large soda costs $2. You and your friend decide to share it. How much does each person pay? (Use division to find the cost per person)

9. **Building Block Bonanza:** You have 8 blocks, your friend has 3, and your sibling has 2. If you combine them all, how many blocks are there in total? (Use addition to find the total number of blocks)

10. **Snack Time Scramble:** A bag of chips costs $1.25, and a juice box costs $0.75. You buy both for a quick snack. If you pay with a $5 bill, how much change do you get back? (Use addition to find the total cost first, then subtraction to find the change)

Remember: BODMAS is your key to mastering Division Dash! So, follow the order, solve correctly, and become a champion!

Chapter 24: Bingo Blitz with the BODMAS Bunch!

The BODMAS Bunch was huddled around a table in their cozy headquarters, looking a little bored. "Math can be fun," declared Miss Addition, ever the optimist, "but sometimes, we all need a break from textbooks."

Captain Bracket stroked his chin. "Agreed, Addition. How about a game that combines our love of math with a little friendly competition?"

A mischievous grin spread across Officer Of's colon-shaped face. "Bingo! But not your ordinary bingo. A BODMAS Bingo Blitz!"

The others cheered. Sergeant Times' muscles tensed with excitement. Even the usually stoic Officer Of seemed to buzz with anticipation.

Miss Addition explained the concept. They would create bingo cards filled with BODMAS equations instead of numbers. To win, a player would need to solve the equations on their card and mark them off as they got the correct answers.

Calling all Bingo Brains!

Get ready for your own BODMAS Bingo Blitz with the BODMAS Bunch!

What you'll need:

- Bingo card printables (one for each player) with BODMAS equations in each square (see below for suggestions). You can also create your own bingo cards!
- Counters or small objects to mark the squares (beans, buttons, etc.)
- Answer sheet with the solutions to the BODMAS equations (optional)

Bingo Card Suggestions:

- **Easy:**
    - $(2 + 3) \times 1 = ?$
    - $10 / 5 = ?$
    - $8 - 2 = ?$
    - $4 + 1 = ?$
    - $3 \times 3 = ?$
- **Medium:**
    - $(5 + 2) \times 4 = ?$
    - $18 / 3 = ?$
    - $12 - (2 \times 2) = ?$
    - $(7 / 1) + 3 = ?$
    - $9 \times 2 = ?$
- **Hard:**
    - $(10 / 2) + (3 \times 2) = ?$
    - $20 - (5 / 5) = ?$
    - $(4 \times 2) - 3 = ?$

- ○ $(8 / 2) + 1 = ?$
- ○ $(3 + 4) \times 2 = ?$

How to play:

1. Each player gets a BODMAS Bingo card.
2. The caller (chosen by players) draws problem cards with BODMAS equations written on them (or reads them aloud from a list).
3. Players solve the BODMAS equation on the caller's card and check their bingo card to see if they have the matching equation.
4. If a player has the equation, they mark it off on their card with a counter.
5. The first player to mark off a complete row, column, or diagonal wins the game!

Bonus Challenge: Can you create your own BODMAS Bingo card with a mix of difficulty levels?

You can even design the layout of your card with fun shapes or colors!

With BODMAS Bingo, you can have a blast practicing your math skills and calling out "Bingo!" with the BODMAS Bunch!

Let Us Learn the Lesson

Bingo Blitz with the BODMAS Bunch: A Fun and Frenzied Math Face-Off!

Calling all math whizzes and BODMAS (PEMDAS in some countries) enthusiasts!

Get ready for Bingo Blitz with the BODMAS Bunch, a fast-paced and exciting game that combines bingo with everyone's favorite math superhero – BODMAS!

Bingo Blitz with the BODMAS Bunch is a game where you'll test your BODMAS knowledge, calculation skills, and a little bit of luck!

Here's how to play:

1. **Gather Your BODMAS Bunch:** This game can be played with classmates, friends, or family. The more players, the merrier!
2. **BODMAS Bingo Boards:** Each player gets a bingo board with empty squares. These squares will have different math problems written on them, involving addition, subtraction, multiplication, and division.
3. **The Caller with the BODMAS Ball:** One person acts as the caller. They'll have a set of cards with BODMAS problems written on them, or they can generate problems on the spot.
4. **Listen Up and Solve!** The caller reads out a BODMAS problem. Everyone solves the problem on their bingo board.
5. **Mark Your Board!** If a player finds the answer to the problem on their bingo board, they mark that square.
6. **Bingo Blitz!** The first player to mark a complete row, column, or diagonal on their board shouts "Bingo Blitz!" and wins!

Adding a Twist: BODMAS Bonus!

- **Double Trouble:** The caller can announce "Double Trouble!" The first player to solve the problem and call out the answer correctly gets to mark two squares on their board!
- **Tricky BODMAS:** The caller can announce "Tricky BODMAS!" The problem will involve multiple operations, and players need to use BODMAS correctly to get the answer.

Benefits of Bingo Blitz with the BODMAS Bunch:

- **Makes learning BODMAS fun and engaging:** Transforms

practice problems into a game.

- **Improves problem-solving skills:** Requires quick thinking and applying BODMAS in a fast-paced environment.
- **Encourages mental math:** Players can practice solving problems without relying on calculators.
- **Provides a social learning experience:** Playing with others can boost engagement and friendly competition.

So grab your BODMAS thinking caps, gather your friends, and get ready for a thrilling Bingo Blitz! It's a guaranteed brain workout and a whole lot of math fun!

Bonus Tip: You can create your own BODMAS Bingo boards with different difficulty levels or find pre-made boards online.

Check Your Basic Knowledge

BODMAS Bingo Blitz: Calling All Math Masters!

Get ready for a BODMAS Bingo bonanza!

Use your BODMAS superpowers to solve problems and be the first to yell "Bingo Blitz!"

Let's Play Bingo Blitz!

Here are some sample problems you might find on your BODMAS Bingo board:

1. **Problem:** 2 + 3 x 4 (Solve: Multiply first! 2 + 12 = 14)
2. **Problem:** (5 - 1) x 3 (Solve: Solve the brackets first! 4 x 3 = 12)
3. **Problem:** 8 / 2 + 1 (Solve: Division first! 4 + 1 = 5)
4. **Problem:** 4 x (2 + 1) (Solve: Solve the brackets first! 4 x 3 = 12)
5. **Problem:** 7 - 3 x 1 (Solve: Multiplication first! 7 - 3 = 4)
6. **Problem:** 10 + 5 / 2 (Solve: Division first! 10 + 2.5 = 12.5)
7. **Problem:** 6 x 2 - 3 (Solve: Multiplication first! 12 - 3 = 9)
8. **Problem:** 12 / 3 + 4 (Solve: Division first! 4 + 4 = 8)

9. **Problem:** 3 + 1 x 5 (Solve: Multiplication first! 3 + 5 = 8)
10. **Problem:** (9 - 2) x 1 (Solve: Solve the brackets first! 7 x 1 = 7)

Ready to play Bingo Blitz?

Sharpen your BODMAS skills, solve problems quickly, and be the first to shout "Bingo Blitz!" Remember, BODMAS is your key to victory!

Chapter 25: The Ultimate BODMAS Challenge!

The BODMAS Bunch was relaxing in their headquarters after a whirlwind week of adventures. Suddenly, the holographic communicator crackled to life. It was Professor Brainiac, their old friend and a renowned mathematician.

"Greetings, BODMAS Bunch!" boomed Professor Brainiac's voice. "I have a challenge for your brilliant minds. A complex problem that requires mastery of BODMAS!"

Miss Addition's eyes lit up. Sergeant Times cracked his knuckles, eager for a mental workout. Officer Of's colon pulsed with anticipation.

Professor Brainiac explained the situation. A vital energy core on a remote space station was malfunctioning. To fix it, they needed to input a specific code, but the code was hidden within a complex equation:

$$[(15 / 3) \times 4] - \{(2 + 8) / 2\} + [5 \times (7 - 1)]$$

"Only a true BODMAS master can solve this equation and reveal the hidden code," Professor Brainiac declared.

Without hesitation, the BODMAS Bunch sprang into action. Miss Addition, ever the strategist, carefully analyzed the equation. "Remember, folks," she reminded them, "BODMAS dictates the order of operations. We need to follow it meticulously."

With Officer of meticulously checking their calculations and Sergeant Times cheering them on, Miss Addition tackled the equation step by step:

Step 1: Division $(15 / 3) = 5$

Step 2: Brackets (Multiplication) $5 \times 4 = 20$

Step 3: Brackets (Addition) $2 + 8 = 10 \, (10 / 2) = 5$

Step 4: Multiplication $5 \times (7 - 1) = 5 \times 6 = 30$

Step 5: Subtraction (work from left to right) $20 - 5 + 30 = 45$

The hidden code was 45!

With a triumphant cheer, the BODMAS Bunch relayed the code to Professor Brainiac.

Moments later, a message arrived from the space station. The code worked! The energy core was back online, and the station was saved.

Professor Brainiac's voice boomed with gratitude. "Congratulations, BODMAS Bunch!

You've proven yourselves true masters of order and operation!"

From that day on, the BODMAS Bunch became legendary throughout the galaxy. Their adventures reminded everyone that with a strong grasp of BODMAS, even the most complex challenges could be solved.

Activity: Become a BODMAS Master!

Calling all junior math whizzes!

Are you ready to become a true BODMAS Master like the BODMAS Bunch?

What you'll need:

- Worksheet with a mix of challenging BODMAS problems (see below for examples).

BODMAS Master Challenge Problems:

- $[(8 / 2) + (3 \times 4)] - (10 / 5) = ?$
- $[5 \times (9 - 2)] / (4 - 1) = ?$
- $[(12 / 3) \times 2] + (7 - 1) = ?$
- $[10 - (3 + 1)] \times 4 = ?$
- $[(6 / 2) + 5] \times (8 - 3) = ?$

How to play:

1. Grab your pencil and paper (or the worksheet) and get ready to solve some challenging BODMAS problems!
2. Remember the BODMAS order of operations: Brackets, Of (Multiplication and Division - solve from left to right), Multiplication and Division (solve from left to right), Addition and Subtraction (solve from left to right).
3. Solve each problem carefully, following the BODMAS order.
4. Once you've solved all the problems, check your answers (answer sheet provided by a grown-up or found online).
5. If you got all the answers correct, congratulations! You are a true BODMAS Master!

Bonus Challenge: Can you create your own BODMAS challenge problems?

Write down a few problems that involve all the BODMAS operations and challenge your friends or family to solve them!

Let Us Learn the Lesson

The Ultimate BODMAS Challenge is a thrilling test of your math skills, designed to make mastering BODMAS fun and exciting!

The Ultimate BODMAS Challenge can take different forms:

- **Individual Puzzle:** You might face a complex equation with a mix of operations, requiring you to use BODMAS correctly to reach the answer.
- **Timed Competition:** You could compete against others, solving multiple BODMAS problems within a limited time. The fastest person with all answers correct wins!
- **Problem-Solving Relay Race:** Teams take turns solving parts of a BODMAS equation, passing the "answer baton" to the next teammate. Teamwork and BODMAS mastery are key!

What makes it "Ultimate"?:

- **Tricky Twists:** The problems could involve missing information, require creative thinking, or have unusual combinations of operations to test your BODMAS knowledge beyond basic scenarios.
- **Multiple Levels:** The challenge can be adapted to different difficulty levels, catering to beginners and BODMAS masters alike.
- **Interactive Elements:** The challenge could be presented in a game format, with visual aids, or even involve physical movement to represent the operations (e.g., jumping for multiplication, spinning for division).

Benefits of The Ultimate BODMAS Challenge:

- **Makes learning BODMAS engaging:** Transforms drills into a fun challenge.
- **Improves problem-solving skills:** Requires critical thinking and applying BODMAS accurately under pressure.
- **Boosts mental math:** Encourages quick thinking and calculation without relying on calculators.

- **Provides a competitive learning environment:** Can spark friendly competition and a sense of accomplishment.

So, are you ready for The Ultimate BODMAS Challenge?
Sharpen your skills, embrace the challenge, and become a true BODMAS champion!

Check Your Basic Knowledge

Let's see if you can conquer these challenges!

1. **Movie Marathon Mayhem:** The movie is 120 minutes long, but you take a 20-minute break in the middle. How long is the total watch time? (**Solve:** Use subtraction first! 120 minutes - 20 minutes = 100 minutes)

2. **Pizza Party Perplexion:** You have 3 slices of pizza, and your friend has 2. You decide to share another whole pizza (8 slices) equally. How many slices do you each have in total now? (**Solve:** Use multiplication first to find the total slices shared (8 x 2 = 16 slices). Then add the slices you already had (16 slices + 3 slices + 2 slices = 21 slices total. Divide by the number of people (21 slices / 2 people = 10.5 slices per person) - Round to the nearest whole number since you can't have half a slice!)

3. **Tricky Treats Trouble:** You have a bag of 15 candies. You give 3 to each of your 2 friends. How many candies are leftover for you? (**Solve:** Use multiplication first to find the total candies given away (3 candies/friend x 2 friends = 6 candies). Then subtract the candies given away from the total (15 candies - 6 candies = 9 candies leftover)

4. **Juice Box Juggle:** There are 6 juice boxes. You drink 2 right away, then buy 4 more. How many juice boxes do you have in total now? (**Solve:** Use subtraction first to find the remaining juice boxes after drinking (6 juice boxes - 2 juice boxes = 4 juice boxes). Then add the juice boxes you bought (4 juice

boxes + 4 juice boxes = 8 juice boxes total)

5. **Sock Sale Surprise:** Socks are originally $5 per pair, but they are on sale for buy 2 pairs, get 1 free. If you buy 2 pairs, what is the total cost? (**Solve:** This one's tricky! Think about how many pairs you get for the sale price. It's like buying 3 pairs for the price of 2. So, divide the original price by the number of pairs you pay for ($5/pair x 2 pairs = $10). You're basically getting 1 pair for free!)

6. **Friendship Bracelet Bonanza!** Craft supplies cost $8. You already saved $4. Do you have enough money to buy the supplies? (**Solve:** Use subtraction to find the remaining amount needed ($8 - $4 = $4). Since $4 is less than what you have saved, you have enough money!)

7. **Sharing Soda Sprint:** A large soda costs $3. You and your friend decide to share it. How much does each person pay? (**Solve:** Use division to find the cost per person ($3 / 2 people = $1.50 per person)

8. **Building Block Bonanza:** You have 6 blocks, your friend has 4, and your sibling has 3. If you combine them all, how many blocks are there in total? (**Solve:** Use addition to find the total number of blocks (6 blocks + 4 blocks + 3 blocks = 13 blocks)

9. **Snack Time Scramble:** A bag of chips costs $1.25, and a juice box costs $0.75. You buy both for a quick snack. If you pay with a $5 bill, how much change do you get back? (**Solve:** First find the total cost of the snacks ($1.25 + $0.75 = $2.00). Then subtract the total cost from the money you paid ($5 - $2.00 = $3.00 in change)

10. **Mystery Movie Mix-Up:** The movie starts at 2:00 pm, and it's 1 hour and 35 minutes long. At what time will the movie end? (**Solve:** Remember, BODMAS doesn't apply here because we're not performing calculations with multiple

operations. We simply need to add the movie duration (1 hour and 35 minutes) to the start time (2:00 pm). Answer: The movie will end at 3:35 pm (2:00 pm + 1 hour 35 minutes = 3:35 pm).

Congratulations!

You've tackled these BODMAS challenges and are well on your way to becoming a BODMAS master!

Remember, practice and perseverance are key to conquering any BODMAS problem. Keep challenging yourself and have fun!

Bonus Chapter: Unleash Your Inner BODMAS Hero!

The BODMAS Bunch are on vacation, but trouble seems to find them wherever they go!

This time, they're visiting the incredible Planet Polygonia, a world filled with geometric shapes and mathematical marvels.

Help the BODMAS Bunch solve a brand new adventure!

Story Template:

As Captain Bracket, Miss Addition, Sergeant Times, and Officer Of explored Polygonia, they stumbled upon a strange sight. A giant cube-shaped building, the Museum of Math Marvels, was shrouded in a mysterious force field!

Suddenly, a holographic message flickered into existence. It was Professor Polyhedron, the museum's curator!

"Greetings, BODMAS Bunch!" boomed Professor Polyhedron's voice. "Our museum is locked down!

To deactivate the force field, you must solve a series of BODMAS challenges scattered throughout the museum."

Your Challenge

Here's where you come in! Help the BODMAS Bunch solve the challenges and save the Museum of Math Marvels!

Write your own BODMAS problems (at least 3) in the spaces below, following the BODMAS order of operations (Brackets, Order (Multiplication and Division - solve from left to right), Multiplication and Division (solve from left to right), Addition and Subtraction (solve from left to right)).

Challenge 1

To unlock the entrance to the museum, the BODMAS Bunch needs to solve a problem displayed on a giant calculator door. Write your BODMAS problem here:

Challenge 2

Inside the museum, the BODMAS Bunch encounters a puzzle wall with various geometric shapes. To pass through, they need to find the shape with the answer to another BODMAS problem. Write your BODMAS problem here:

Challenge 3

Finally, the BODMAS Bunch reaches the control room, where a final challenge awaits. They need to enter the correct code to deactivate the force field. This code is the answer to a complex BODMAS equation! Write your BODMAS problem (with the answer being the code) here:

The End?

Will the BODMAS Bunch solve all your challenges and save the Museum of Math Marvels?

Use your imagination to complete the story!

Bonus Activity:

Once you've written your challenges, try solving them yourself!

Can you crack the code and become a hero alongside the BODMAS Bunch?

You can also share your challenges and stories with friends and family to create even more BODMAS adventures!

Don't miss out!

Visit the website below and you can sign up to receive emails whenever Rekha Kumari publishes a new book. There's no charge and no obligation.

https://books2read.com/r/B-A-QAJFB-RSRAD

BOOKS 2 READ

Connecting independent readers to independent writers.

Did you love *BODMAS Blast Off: A Fun Way to Master Maths*? Then you should read *A.I. Academy: Where Robots Learn Kindness*[1] by Rekha Kumari!

[2]

A.I. Academy: Where Robots Learn Kindness

Calling all curious minds!

Dive into the exciting world of the A.I. Academy with Bolt, a kindhearted robot on a journey of discovery. This delightful children's book is packed with fun, adventure, and valuable lessons that will resonate with readers of all ages.

Here's what makes Bolt Learns About Kindness a must-read:

A heartwarming story about friendship and acceptance: Join Bolt and his fellow robots as they navigate the complexities of emotions, communication, and teamwork. Witness the power of friendship

---

1. https://books2read.com/u/4Djo1r

2. https://books2read.com/u/4Djo1r

blossom as they learn to appreciate each other's unique strengths and embrace their differences.**AI portrayed in a positive light:** This book breaks away from stereotypical portrayals of AI. Instead, it highlights the potential for robots to be kind, helpful, and positive members of society.**Interactive learning through engaging activities:** Bolt and his classmates participate in exciting simulations and challenges that bring the concepts of kindness, empathy, and responsible communication to life.**Actionable takeaways for young readers:** Each chapter concludes with an "Actionable Activity" section, encouraging children to put the book's lessons into practice. These activities spark creativity, promote kindness in their communities, and inspire a sense of global citizenship.**Beautifully written with a positive message:** Simple, easy-to-understand language and vivid descriptions make this book enjoyable for young readers. The core message of kindness and using your abilities for good leaves a lasting impression.

More than just a story, Bolt Learns About Kindness is a valuable tool for parents and educators looking to:
Spark children's interest in artificial intelligence and its potential benefits.Foster discussions about emotions, empathy, and responsible communication.Encourage teamwork and appreciation for diversity.Promote acts of kindness in everyday life.

Join Bolt on his heartwarming journey and discover the power of AI for good!

Also by Rekha Kumari

Grandma's Time Machine: An Adventure Through History
A.I. Academy: Where Robots Learn Kindness
BODMAS Blast Off: A Fun Way to Master Maths

About the Author

Rekha Kumari is a dynamic and accomplished individual, embodying the roles of both an expert entrepreneur and a passionate educator. With a wealth of experience in both fields, she has dedicated her life to empowering children and guiding them towards success.

As a seasoned entrepreneur, Rekha has navigated the complexities of the business world with finesse. Her innovative ideas, strategic vision, and unwavering determination have enabled her to establish herself as a leader in her industry. Through her ventures, she has not only achieved significant professional milestones but has also served as an inspiration to aspiring entrepreneurs, especially women, encouraging them to pursue their dreams fearlessly.

In addition to her entrepreneurial endeavors, Rekha is deeply committed to education and believes in the transformative power it holds. As a teacher, she goes beyond imparting knowledge; she nurtures young minds, instilling in them the values of resilience, determination, and excellence. Her teaching philosophy revolves around building strong foundations and fostering a growth mindset, equipping her students with the tools they need to become winners in life.

Rekha Kumari's unique blend of entrepreneurial acumen and educational expertise makes her a sought-after figure in both business and academic circles. Her dedication to empowering the next generation underscores her belief in the limitless potential of every child. Through her guidance and mentorship, she continues to shape future leaders and pave the way for a brighter tomorrow.